Bounce

Be Transformed

*Change your mind,
Change your life,
Change the world!*

Lana Ribble Staheli, Ph.D.

*Profits from the sale of this book go toward making it available
free of charge on our website, Bouncebetransformed.com.
Scholarships to **Bounce Seminars** and **Bounce Circles**
are also available at no cost.*

Bounce, Be Transformed

© 2008 by Lana Ribble Staheli

Notice of Rights

All rights reserved. No part of this book may be reproduced or transmitted in any form or by any means electronic, mechanical, photocopying, recording or otherwise without the prior written permission of the author. For information on getting permission for reprints or excerpts, e-mail bouncebetransformed@gmail.com.

Trademarks

Bounce, Be Transformed and its logo are trademarks of Lana Ribble Staheli in the United States and/or other countries.

ISBN 978-1-60458-393-9

Printed and bound in the United States of America
by CCS Printing, Bellevue, WA

Editor: Judy Dreis
Cover Design: Angela Turk

To Order Books

To order copies of *Bounce, Be Transformed*, e-mail bouncebetransformed@gmail.com; visit our website at bouncebetransformed.com; or Google us.

Introduction

Lana Ribble Staheli is a unique individual with both a huge heart and intellect. You don't have to take my word for it. Just open this book and her wisdom and soul become quickly apparent. Lana has pulled together her experience as a counselor, therapist and life coach to create Bounce, a simple but profound program to add joy and fulfillment to our lives. Her voice shines through this book and encourages us to be the best person we can be—and she convinces us that we are pretty damn good if we just embrace life and understand our possibilities.

Lana's gift is her ability to help and guide us. The challenges of life are neither small nor fleeting, but Lana has the ability to take tightly wrapped problems and make them clearer and more manageable. She excavates our thoughts and feelings and how they interact with our behavior. She helps us figure out how to reconfigure our approach to life by helping us understand our emotional blocks, our deepest desires, and our core fears. No matter how secure our emotional vault is, she helps us open it up and be transformed to who we want to be and what we want to do. She gives us tools to reframe our thinking so that we can use our new perspective to make life exponentially better.

Lana's lazer-like insight and practical wisdom make us look at our world in a new way. With the benefit of this simple but inspirational book, we can be the architect of our own more effective and happy life. Lana's wish is to "give back"—What a gift!

Pepper Schwartz, Ph.D., Professor of Sociology, University of Washington
and author, *Prime: Adventures and Advice on Sex, Love, and the Sensual Years*

*For all the women who **Bounce**, present and future!*

1 *Bounce*—And How It All Began	2
2 *Bounce* – Be Transformed	10
3 *Bounce* Toward Being Your Best	16
4 Transition to Transformation	40
5 Stages of Transition	56
6 Core Emotions	80
7 Core Needs	86
8 Endorphins—Nature's Miracle Drugs	100
9 *Bounce Basics* for the Mind and Body	114
10 Sleep—A *Bounce Basic*	122
11 Meditation—A *Bounce Basic*	128
12 Brain Training—A *Bounce Basic*	134
13 The ABCs of MENTAL	144
14 *Bounce* Transformations	188

Bounce—And How It All Began

It was three or four years ago that I decided I had to write about what I had learned over the past 35 years coaching and counseling highly successful men and women. I wrote **Bounce** to make the practical wisdom I have gained available to everyone at little or no cost. It is my effort to give back to a universe that has been very generous to me.

I have seen extraordinarily talented and successful people in my practice, and I am grateful for all I have learned. I think my clients have been unusually successful in part because they are willing to change. They believe in the importance of personal growth through learning and experimenting with new ways of doing things. They are willing to live in the present and move through difficulties without dragging the past with them. We all have extraordinary abilities and the key to having an happy, successful life is living in a way that allows us to be our personal best.

As I put the book together I wanted to be sure that what I suggested was useful and effective. I invited a group of women to get together and talk about our need for change. Our lives were good, but not great, and we wanted more challenge or growth. We wanted to be living our lives at our best—learning, growing and transforming. We didn't want to coast. Coasting only works going downhill. We wanted lives filled with joy and meaning. We wanted **Bounce!**

Other women heard about our little "circle" and wanted to join. Soon we realized we had tapped an unmet need: the need for connection with other women who held similar values, to focus on our strengths and move toward creating lives of joy and fulfillment. We certainly hadn't expected to ignite grass-roots enthusiasm with **Bounce,** but we did. We set up a small event for 20 to 25 women whom we thought of as like-minded and who would be willing to try something new. Our inaugural event was held in Seattle on October 29, 2007. In keeping with my desire to make the ideas of Bounce accessible to everyone, there was no charge for the **Bounce** Seminars or Circles. Eighty women attended—76 of whom signed up for the next **Bounce** meeting. **Bounce, Be Transformed** was launched.

*Eighty women showed up at our first **Bounce** meeting.*

Bounce started as an idea that transformed into a movement. We focused the events on women because we believe the world will benefit from more female influence that will come from the unique networks that women can build with each other. Women's intuitive way of finding creative solutions to problems can help make the world safer and healthier. Women's work as caregivers and nurturers could eliminate world hunger. Women's work as homemakers can lead to restoring the global environment. Women's work of teaching people to understand one another can lead to world peace. But women's work is also about having fun while seeking both joy and meaning.

Another facet of *Bounce* is that we all enjoy and appreciate men. We live in a very rich country with many privileges, largely because of the work and values of men. Each of us has men—husbands, fathers, sons, brothers, friends and relatives—whom we love and respect. Using *Bounce* principles, we want to learn how to be with men in even more inspired and loving ways.

Change does not need to be difficult or gut-wrenching. In fact, changing ourselves can be fun, especially when we blend our energy with that of others. *Bounce* is a simple and fun approach to life. It is based on the belief that by changing our thinking, focusing on creating joy and meaning, we can live in a process of ongoing transformation, becoming our best and inspiring others to become their best. We can change our minds, our lives, and the world!

The beauty of *Bounce* is its simplicity—anyone can *Bounce!* People can learn to *Bounce* from reading this book, attending our Seminars or creating their own *Bounce* Circles. The entire contents of the book are available at no cost on our website, Bouncebetransformed.com.

Eight women have taken *Bounce* from an idea about how to be their personal best to a guide for you. Like everyone, we have each hit something hard in life and we have bounced! In these difficult economic times, the best investment we can make is in ourselves. Bounce teaches you how to make some simple day to day changes you will help you to be your best and in so doing change the world, one day at a time.

Join us and bring *Bounce* into *your* world. Simply change your mind, change your life and change the world.

THE BOUNCE WOMEN

Ranging in age from 45 to 75, the *Bounce* women have diverse backgrounds and common beliefs. We all believe in living life as a journey of growth and transformation. We believe life is to be enjoyed, and at the same time we are determined to contribute to the world around us.

Susan, a former Playboy bunny, body-builder, and organizational consultant, faced two enormous setbacks in her mid-40s: a head injury as a result of an automobile accident and the death of her husband while they were on a scuba diving trip in the Caribbean. She is now preparing for a body-building competition at the age of 58. She sits on the board of Global-HELP, an organization that makes children's medical research available to doctors in developing countries free of charge.

Katherine, an artist and sculptress, found herself divorced and broke at the age of 30. She worked creating lost cast sculptures until she became ill from the toxins in the materials. She is now 59 and remarried. She, her son and husband have designed and built an energy-independent home and studio. Together they design jewelry that is currently sold at the Museum of Modern Art in Chicago, New York's MOMA, and others.

Patricia, a mechanical and nuclear engineer, waited till her late 30s to marry, inheriting two stepchildren. Her husband had a dream of owning his own business and she decided to support his dream, agreeing to sign for loans. After 10 years of marriage, he told her it was over, there was someone else. She was shocked but even more distressed when she discovered she was responsible for all the business debt. Patricia lost her anger, and gained compassion, walking 600 miles in preparation for the Susan G. Komen 3-Day Walk for the Cure® breast cancer fundraiser. She considers it one of the most fulfilling experiences of her life. She bounced further, changing jobs from a company where good relationships were not important to a company that places a high value on relationships within and outside the company.

Sarah, a 51-year-old accountant, was surprised to discover that her husband of 27 years who had wanted a divorce to "discover" himself actually had a one-year-old son. Sarah decided to stop grieving and start bouncing, transforming herself by writing a book, *Play the Real Life Money Game with Your Teen*. She is now a talk show regular and expert on kids and money.

Pepper, professor of sociology at the University of Washington, is a divorced mother of two and world-renowned sociologist who recently published her autobiography, *Prime: Adventures and Advice on Sex, Love and the Sensual Years*. At 64, Pepper teaches, speaks and writes on relationships and sexuality.

Elizabeth, at 75, is a single, independent woman who loves playing golf and raising two of her granddaughters. As a very young child, Elizabeth developed life-threatening asthma and allergies that led to a very sheltered childhood, leaving her unprepared to cope with a physically and emotionally abusive husband. She has pioneered a research endowment at Seattle Children's Hospital for investigation into childhood asthma and allergies.

Angela, 45, a former beauty queen, found herself a single mother of two young boys when her husband decided to leave. She created a successful business as a graphic designer and now has her own firm. Angela designed the book cover and *Bounce* logo and stationery.

Looking at these pictures you can see that each woman is beautiful, but as you read *Bounce*, you will see that we didn't always look this way. You can read the stories of some of the *Bounce* women later, but first I'll tell you about myself.

1. Susan
2. Katherine
3. Lana
4. Patricia
5. Sarah
6. Pepper
7. Elizabeth
8. Angela

Originally our group numbered 11. Jennifer and Bradie lived in another city and wrote 2 books for parents. Debbie, our 11th member, died suddenly at age 50, shortly after her first meeting with us.

My First Bounce

Dr. Munger walked into the room looking down at the chart; he spoke quietly, my mother recalls. "Lana is one of the prettiest babies I have ever seen—but there is something very wrong." She doesn't remember what he said after that. Her baby was being moved to the University Hospital. "You can see her later," the doctor promised, "but she has to go now." My father and mother, Vercil and Mildred Ribble, married in 1944 when he came home on shore leave from the Navy. They had come to know one another through their wartime letters. By 1945 they had purchased their first home, and my father worked at Consumer's Power Company where he would work his entire life. He was a lineman, climbing electrical poles to string power lines to people's homes. My mother, Mildred, had worked at Eaton Manufacturing during and after the war, but quit before I was born.

On June 21, 1947, I was born, weighing 6 pounds and 12 ounces, and on June 24 I was admitted to the University of Michigan Department of Pediatrics where I would spend most of the next eight months of my life. Dr. Munger had made the correct diagnosis of TracheoEsophageal Fistula, or TEF.

My parents, Vercil and Mildred Ribble

"Lana is one of the prettiest babies I have ever seen, but there is something very wrong."

TEF is an opening between the swallowing tube (esophagus) and the windpipe (trachea) that allows anything swallowed to go into the lungs. Plus, my esophagus came to an abrupt end. Most babies died from suffocation within hours.

On June 25, at four days old, my first of six surgeries was performed by Drs. Cameron Haight and William Lees. Dr. Haight was the first surgeon to develop a way of closing the windpipe and feeding the baby through its esophagus. TEF was a fatal birth defect often because it was part of a syndrome that included other defects. Like myself, most babies born with TEF have lung, spine, heart, or kidney problems. Anesthesia for babies was new and largely guesswork; antibiotics were untested on babies; and doctors had little success with surgeries on infants, but I was fortunate. I was three months old when I left the hospital for the first time. I would return biweekly to have my esophagus dilated.

Mildred with Lana at 3 months old.

Lana Sue Ribble

A week after my discharge, my mother and grandmother took me back to the hospital for a routine procedure to dilate my esophagus. The young resident doctor accidentally ruptured my esophagus while attempting to enlarge it. The pediatric team continued to try to open my esophagus for the next 48 hours before calling the surgeon. By the time Drs. Haight and Lees saw me, I was dying. My esophagus had completely closed and I had an lung infection.

Over the course of the next month I gained enough strength for Dr. Haight to experiment with a new surgical procedure. Although I survived the surgery, I had contracted pneumonia and a wound infection. My right lung collapsed, leading to more surgeries. I had been getting large doses of the then-new antibiotic, penicillin, since birth, but now the infection in my lungs was resistant to one of the only antibiotics on the market.

I was nearly six months old and a mere five pounds when Dr. Lees suggested an experimental antibiotic, streptomycin, which had never been prescribed to an infant. Streptomycin was known to cause blindness and deafness, but my parents gave their consent in the hope of saving my life. A few days before Christmas, with my lung completely collapsed, I bounced back.

In February 1948 I went home to stay. I went back and forth to the hospital, but I was mostly at home. A year later, Dr. Lees wrote, "I sincerely believe that from now on we must treat Lana as though she were a normal child, which she appears to be." His words have always resonated with me. I believed I was normal despite having an abnormal spine, limited lung capacity, irregular heartbeat and an esophagus one-quarter of normal size.

There were many more trips back to the University of Michigan for me, but they were simply part of my "normal" life. I have always lived with these issues and have learned to work around them. Believing I was normal shaped my life.

Mildred holding Lana at 6 months old, weighing 5 pounds

"I sincerely believe that from now on we must treat Lana as though she were an entirely normal child, which she apparently appears to be. I, too, was delighted to hear that your Christmas this past year was so wonderful. I can recall distinctly spending a good share of last Christmas with Lana here at the hospital."
Sincerely,
Dr. William Lees

One of my great pleasures is travel. My husband, Lynn, and I have visited 70 to 80 different countries. A physician friend who treats children with my disability was surprised we traveled so extensively with my limitations. Then he added, "I guess it was OK as long as you stayed in major metropolitan areas with good health care readily available."

I chuckled as I thought about our "around the world" trip when I was carrying a 25-pound backpack and staying in minus-4-star hotels; hiking with Nadire and Selim in Santorini; trekking the mountain trails in New Zealand; going by train with one tiny bag behind the Iron Curtain; flying into remote rivers to go rafting; taking the Trans-Siberian Railway from Russia to China. There was the time we hiked all day through the jungle, slept in a native home and rode elephants another day before floating in a locally made raft down a river in Thailand. We did all this so Lynn could study the feet of people who had never worn shoes.

It didn't occur to me not to go because I had limitations. I am grateful to my parents that I grew up believing I could do whatever I wanted. An odd twist is that while I believed I could do what I wanted physically, I believed I was *below average* in intelligence. That belief has also shaped my life. I have had many bounces during my life as have all the **Bounce** women. I will tell you our stories, and those of other women who have joined **Bounce** along the way. But first I want to explain the idea behind **Bounce, Be Transformed—Change Your Mind, Change Your Life, Change the World!**

Bounce – Be Transformed

Bounce is a way of life based on commitment to growth and transformation. We can change ourselves and our lives by being intentional in our thoughts and choices, creating lives filled with joy and meaning. We are born with *Bounce*, the ability to grow and change, to continually become better, and to always be in transformation. Life is complex and so are we, but change is natural, and unlike any other being on earth, we can change what we feel, what we believe, and what we do by changing our mind—otherwise we would still be living in a nice little cave somewhere in Africa.

The human brain is highly adaptable, and the newest regions of the brain allow us to compile, sort, and reconfigure what we know. We can change how we think about ourselves and the people around us. We can rethink our past and through our thinking change our future. We can change our minds, our lives, and the world by learning *Bounce*.

Bounce is a way of living that gives us the foundation to create a life based on joy and meaning. It requires only thought and intention—qualities we already possess. We all have *Bounce*; we use it after everyday hassles and inconveniences, and we can bounce and rebound after devastating events. Or at least that is what we are supposed to do, but sometimes with the pace and complexity of life we forget and let little things become too big. We even start to believe that we don't have time to care for ourselves, but we do. All it takes is a little "pruning" to make room. I'll tell you more about pruning later.

Unlike any other being on earth, we can change our lives by intentionally changing our thoughts.

Life is full of surprises, and our need for a rebound bounce is inevitable. Choosing a life based on *Bounce* readies us for those times when powerful forces of circumstance slam us against the wall. When we start with *Bounce*, we can harness the forces of energy that accelerate our descent and use these energies to soar to new heights—heights we have never known.

The speed of our lives moves at a faster clip than at any time in human history. We are bombarded with communication from people down the street and around the world. Cell phones and e-mail connect us to one another like never before.

Airplanes transport us from one side of the country to the other in a matter of hours. And while the Internet broadens our world and our thinking, it also overwhelms our circuits and floods our brains with useful and not so useful information. All too often we get ahead of our capacity to cope and maintain our own equilibrium.

I recently celebrated a milestone birthday and invited 100 friends. My mother later remarked, "I don't think I even know 100 people." I thought back and it is true. In my mother's and grandmother's day, they had large extended families, a few neighbors, and that was it. My mother still has lunch with friends she grew up with over 80 years ago, while I know only a few people who live in the same town where they grew up.

Living life at warp speed leaves us pumped up on our own hormones. For the purpose of *Bounce* we are focusing on steroids and endorphins. Steroids are naturally produced stress hormones. High levels of steroid hormones are linked to ailments that lessen our quality of life and lead to disease and early death. Heart disease, the #1 killer of both men and women, is linked to high levels of steroids. Cancer, stroke, breathing problems, accidents, anorexia, migraines, chronic fatigue, irritable bowel syndrome, obesity and a host of other health problems are all affected by high levels of steroids related to stress.

Stress has become a popular focus over the past few decades. With *Bounce* we believe it is better to focus on what we *do* want—good health. Just try saying aloud, "I feel so stressed." You will notice yourself tense up. Now take a deep breath and say aloud, "I feel relaxed." Don't you feel calmer? Most people do. Our thoughts and words take us toward producing either steroids or endorphins.

Endorphins are hormones that strengthen the immune system, repair cells, relieve pain, counter the effects of stress and delay aging. *Bounce* focuses on creating endorphins to naturally insure our ability to live life at our 90%+ level. Think and talk about being your best and you will begin to be transformed.

Our desire to change and transform ourselves toward being our best is deeply embedded in our nature and is as powerful as our need to eat or sleep. *Bounce, Be Transformed—Change Your Mind, Change Your Life, Change the World!* is a guide for giving your life joy and meaning.

SEEK JOY

Joy is the emotional component and an integral part of **Bounce**. Of the five core emotions—fear, anger, disgust, sadness, and joy—joy is the only one that triggers endorphins. They repair damaged cells, increase the effectiveness of the immune system, relieve pain, restore full brain activity, and slow aging. Endorphins open up the mind, making us ready for new experiences, challenges, and discoveries. They show us the way to be our best.

It is better to focus on seeking joy than thinking about managing your stress. Whatever we focus on we tend to get, so focus on what you want, not what you don't want.

Seeking joy makes **Bounce** fun. Laughing, joking, having play dates, and doing silly things helps us physically as well as mentally. Everything goes better when we are joyful. We take better care of ourselves, get along with others better and have time and energy to find joy and meaning in day-to-day life. People who seek joy are usually happy. Seeking joy and finding happiness is not expensive or difficult. The happiest people do have certain elements in common but they are not what you might expect.

Many myths surround the concept of happiness. Here are a few of the most common:

The quality most Americans believe would make them happy is money. It doesn't! Yes, enough money does make people happier, there is nothing good about poverty, but when a family has an income of $60,000 a year or more, money makes no difference in a person's happiness. Enough is enough.

Marriage? No. Men have better health when they are married and are slightly happier than unattached men, but women are only happy in what they consider a good marriage, and even then there is little difference in the happiness of married and unmarried women.

Some people are just born happy? Not really. There is a very small percent of people who are happy all the time, but overall happiness takes effort and intent. Those who are happy work at being happy.

Good health? Yes, but it is number 11 on the list of the top 15. When happy people are ill, they are likely to make the best of it.

Some people's lives are easier than others? Research has repeatedly shown that happy people and unhappy people have the same life experiences. Happy people's lives are riddled with illness, death, disaster, disappointment, and hardship in the same numbers, and with the same severity as unhappy people. The difference is that happy people recall events and experiences with fondness or humor, or at least with an "oh well" rather than an "oh no."

It is easier to be unhappy than happy? No. Being unhappy is as much work and effort as being happy. It may feel easier just because it is a familiar habit. Unhappy people tell certain experiences over and over with drama, conviction, and intense emotion, as though their experience is of terrible, unjust events rarely experienced by humankind.

They usually think of themselves as innocent victims. Being a victim is a sure-fire way to be unhappy. It takes time and thought to keep up on bad happenings. The truths about how to find happiness are surprising in that they are within anyone's grasp. It is a matter of seeking joy, celebrating everyday successes, and emphasizing the good! Here is what researchers report:

• Small day-to-day pleasures outrank "big bang" events.

• Sex and having fun with friends outranks housework and watching TV. (No surprise there!)

• Having fun is not as important to happiness as helping others.

• The single most important factor in happiness is not what we do, but what we think about what we do, and who we think we are.

We must be conscious of both our internal and external self to have control or choice over what we believe and what we experience. The belief that we are in control of ourselves and that our lives are meaningful is more important than fame, fortune, or fun. Being your best creates the foundation for happiness. The highest paid executive who believes he is entitled to big bucks is less happy than the lowest paid grocery clerk who knows that she is doing her best and that her best is benefiting others.

Our happiness and sense of well-being are normal and healthy aspects of who we are, driven by our innate need for growth and discovery. It is only by knowing and accepting ourselves that we can be our best. Being your best means having self-awareness, an intimate connection with others; the enjoyment of daily life; and living altruistic values.

Five most important qualities for happiness
1. Sense of control over our own life
2. Close connection with other people
3. Meaningful activity benefiting others
4. Passionate work building on strengths
5. Appreciation for self and others' gratitude

It is simple and fun to add joy and pleasure to your life while having a clear sense of what it takes to be the best you can be. ***Bounce*** guides you through this process of growth and discovery, helping you live your life at the highest possible level, knowing that each stage prepares you for the next stage in this endless evolution of self. It is through seeking joy and meaning, being happy and open-minded that we can become our best.

DON'T WORRY, BE HAPPY

Perhaps it is from my childhood that I concluded that I should just have fun and, as the song says, "Don't Worry, Be Happy!" Like everyone else, I have had times in life that are hard, distressing, frightening, or hurtful, and that little piece of advice helps. I have the choice to be happy or unhappy. We all do, so we may as well be happy.

At a 70th birthday party for my husband, Lynn, I gave a presentation, "Travels with Lynn, Facing Death and Life," and this is one of the stories I told.

One of the most memorable adventures I have had with Lynn is a kayaking trip in Prince William Sound, Alaska. I had never been in a kayak, but Lynn organized our trip with a local skipper who took us by powerboat to a remote location, Harriman Fjord. Captain Jay agreed he would pick us up at the same spot in five days. We had a wonderful time, truly alone in the wild with whales, sea otters and calving glaciers. We only saw one other human that week.

The time came to leave so we cleaned up our campsite, tossing out our dehydrated food that we were now sick of eating (my idea). We decided to paddle toward town rather than wait for the pick-up at the appointed spot (not my idea!). "How could they miss us? We have a bright yellow kayak," Lynn reminded me, so off we paddled. It was a gloriously beautiful bright day with the cool aqua-blue water reflecting the pure white mountain snow.

As we paddled around the corner of the inlet, we were suddenly surrounded by a pod of whales, surfacing and diving ahead of us and beside us. Oh! (WOW!); Uh-oh! (glacial water); Oh, well! (die quickly). We floated along, awed by their beauty and grace.

A couple of hours later, we spotted Captain Jay and his boat and we waved happily, but he sped past us. "Oh, well," we thought, "he wasn't looking because he expected us to be where he left us." Soon we saw him speeding toward us. We waved vigorously, knowing he would be looking for us this time, but he sped on by without ever slowing down. We gathered all the dry wood we could find to set a big bonfire, unpacked our emergency kit, and took out our emergency flares. Surely with fire, smoke, and flares, he would see us. But the fire dwindled before igniting and four of the five flares were duds. Early the next morning we heard the hum of a helicopter. "Rescued!" I screamed. But we weren't. No rescue. We had only candy left, and now that old dehydrated food that I had dumped when we left camp didn't sound so bad. We snacked on candy and kept paddling.

There is a near-myth that everything is big in Alaska, including mosquitoes that are the size of birds and that fly in a swarm like locusts. Some of these giant mosquitoes found us. They surrounded Lynn from head to toe while ignoring me completely. I did not have a single bite; Lynn had too many to count. I chuckled, thinking, "This must be cosmic justice."

The next day we saw a group of kayaks. With Lynn's accelerated paddling we reached them and they radioed Captain Jay, who was beyond annoyed. He was getting ready to call for rescue, but I did wonder how long he planned to wait before calling for help. We had missed our flight to Seattle by days, Alaska Airlines honored our ticket and gave us an upgrade I really appreciated.

At the end of my presentation, a friend commented, "I can't believe you went with him on those ill-planned and half-baked vacations." A bit defensively I said, "They weren't really half-baked," but I realized I would not have wanted to miss any of our *half-baked misadventures*. They are some of the happiest and funniest memories I have. I realized too that I could definitely and easily have turned this experience into a very bad memory, or use it to build a case against Lynn. But instead I recall it as fun, exciting, and a bonding experience between us.

Of course, I also told of the time we were driving in Egypt, when I looked up from the map and said to Lynn, "Gosh the map shows the Nile on our left, but looking out the window it is on our right". I had navigated us into the desert. We later found an Egyptian Ferry that floated us back to the other side, where we were taken in by a lovely farming family for the night then directed back to Cairo. Fortunately, Lynn thought that was great—afterwards.

We can think whatever we choose. Life holds many surprises and for me many of these surprises have come when things did not go all that well. I embrace them all. I cannot change the past, but I can choose to be happy in the present moment. Anger simply creates more anger. Worry creates more worry. Happy creates move... happy. Choose happy!

Bounce Toward Being Your Best

Bouncing toward being your best means living your life at your highest standard. I think of it as the 90%+ level. Not striving to be perfect, but intentionally building on the qualities that you like best in ourselves.

We created a list of qualities that define being our best as human beings. We developed this list from surveys by business and professional leaders as well as from the psychological literature. We studied the qualities of "most admired people in the world" and what it means to be "self-actualized."

We then grouped these qualities into four categories: self-awareness; an intimate connection with others; enjoyment of daily life; and living altruistic values. We found that our list matched the qualities expressed by people who are happy. It turns out that when we are being our best, we are also happy and healthy.

This section will explain each of the four growth steps in more detail, and incorporate stories of women who met the challenge of a growth step and moved toward becoming their best.

When we allow ourselves to be joyful and have the experience of living our values, we are able to meet our needs quickly and efficiently, allowing time and energy to bounce from one way of being to another. It is through this process that we create joy and meaning in life—and find happiness. Bounce happily toward being YOUR best.

Growth steps for becoming your best
Self-awareness
An intimate connection with others
Enjoyment of daily life
Living altruistic values

Human life will never be understood unless its highest aspirations are taken into account. Growth, self-actualization, the striving toward health, the quest for identity and autonomy, the yearning for excellence must by now be accepted beyond question as a widespread and perhaps universal human tendency.
—*Abraham Maslow, Ph.D.*

SELF-AWARENESS

Knows beliefs and feelings

Awareness of the perception of others

Committed to ongoing growth and transformation

Finds joy in self without criticism, shame, or regret

Trusts own perceptions

Sees the world realistically

Cares for self physically, emotionally, spiritually

Growth is the journey we take to know ourselves.

Self-awareness means knowing yourself, not necessarily changing yourself, and it certainly does not mean focusing on what is wrong with you. I like Diedre's description of what she learned about self-awareness.

Diedre, a tall, pretty woman in her early 50s and a grandmother of four, works as a bookkeeper. Diedre came to two **Bounce** Circles before her mother became ill. During our first Circle meeting, she decided she wanted to do more for herself and stop worrying about other people. Then her mother had a stroke. Diedre decided to move away from Seattle to be with her mom. She writes, *My (**Bounce** Circle) assignment was not to take on any more projects, but then my mom had a stroke. I have learned that all of my hard work has paid off over the years because I am able to be with her full-time and still keep my job.*

It was a blessing to appreciate this and "cash in," so to speak, on the years of diligence. So in a nutshell, I ended up doing the opposite of the plan, but I still feel in balance. It all just changed form. I'm grateful and I think I'm OK. I definitely got what I needed—an appreciation for what I have and where I am in my life. I thought I had a self-esteem issue, but it turns out I'm just critical of myself at every turn. I'm practicing not doing that so much; accepting my best for what it is.

I learned to appreciate my life as it is. I saw that I have been immensely blessed with love all around me . . . I don't need much other than to learn to take better care of my physical health, and I am reminded daily of the need to exercise more.

Sometimes we are not so far away from being our best as we may think. It is through self-awareness that we find self-acceptance. It is not so much that we need to change *who* we are as it is that we need to accept ourselves *as* we are. It is through the process of looking for and finding the best in ourselves that we become even better. And, as in most other aspects of life, we find what we are looking for—so look for your goodness.

> *It is through self-awareness that we find self-acceptance. It is not so much that we need to change "who" we are as it is that we need to accept ourselves "as" we are.*

21

Self-Acceptance

Self-awareness that leads you to being your best includes self-acceptance. There are two types of self-acceptance. One is the realization of a fact or truth and coming to terms with it. The other is tolerating something without protest. These two types of acceptance take us down entirely different paths.

Lola had struggled with self-acceptance for many years because of her body image. She had gained and lost and gained weight year after year for the last 30 years. She continually worked on her weight, but up and down it went. She had tried every diet, exercised daily and fought with herself continually. She decided that she should just accept her obesity and live with it, so she resigned herself to being "fat and frumpy," but she just couldn't believe that she had to be fat. This is Lola's story.

I have always been open to the idea of weight loss surgery. I never thought of it as a reality because I was one of those people who was fat but not fat enough. For most obesity surgeries you have to be 100 pounds overweight, and I was usually about 60 to 80 pounds over. I thought maybe I should gain 40 pounds to be fat enough, but I couldn't do that to myself.

A girlfriend, Darlene, who was about the same weight as me, started losing. We got together a couple times a month, and like me she had been on lots of diets. So when I first noticed her getting thinner, I thought it was just another diet. But, the next time I saw her she had lost 50 to 60 pounds, so I asked her, "What's the deal here?"

She quietly shared her secret. She wanted me to have the same success, but she didn't want to blab to everybody. She had had surgery. She told me about her surgery and gave me the website information. I read it and saw the $17,000 cost and put it aside.

I thought it wasn't possible for me, but over the next year I gained more weight despite my best efforts. Every time I saw Darlene, I felt sick. "She looks so good, that could be me," I thought. I had been dieting for 30 years, and my weight went up and up. I was reaching menopause and I knew my weight would just keep going up. I needed to do something drastic and I needed to do it now.

I started researching all options and thought my best choice was to have surgery. I asked my sister, who is a nurse, what she thought of the surgery. She thought it was a good idea. She had watched me struggle year after year. Talking to someone about it made me think maybe it was possible. I talked to my husband and he was supportive but noncommittal. If I wanted to do it, it would be up to me.

I read testimonials from other patients. Everyone said "This is just a tool. You have to do the work to be healthy." The more I studied I realized surgery was not an easy way out. My mind volleyed back and forth, "Have it done, spend the money, take the chance or wait and try the newest diet; maybe I hadn't tried everything."

I was tired of going back and forth. I thought, "It is so expensive and complicated, maybe it was just not meant to be." I asked God if I was doing my will instead of His. I asked God to guide me by letting things fall into place or by creating more obstacles, one way or the other. I know from experience that when I try too hard and nothing works, it is just not meant to be.

Bit by bit everything seemed to fall into place. I took on an extra job and saved every penny. I didn't spend an extra dime anywhere. I saved $8,000, so I was less than halfway there, but saving the other half seemed a long ways away. Then my sister offered to loan me the rest.

There was still more work to do. I had to qualify for the surgery. There were lots of hoops to jump through. I had to meet with 10 people who had had the surgery, fill out a detailed life history, including a psychological assessment. I needed my doctor's permission since she would be doing the follow-up. And my family had to agree, including a notarized letter from my husband agreeing to support my surgery. There seemed to be an endless number of forms to fill out to even be considered for the surgery.

I finished my 20-page assessment, including the psychological assessment, and sent it in. I waited. A week later, I got the call. I was eligible for the surgery. My mind was made up, I wanted to do it. I scheduled my operation for three weeks later. My sister came with me. I was excited as I thought of having one-size clothes in my closet and being able to buy nice things, knowing I would never get fat again. I had always wanted to work for a nonprofit and do something that makes a difference, but I couldn't bring myself to apply as a fat woman.

I knew I wouldn't waste this opportunity. I knew how to eat right after dieting for so many years and I liked the "good" foods. A downside of the surgery is that I won't be able to eat as much and maybe I won't be able to eat some of the foods I like. Then there was the risk of the surgery itself. I could die if things went bad or maybe end up with a worse problem. I might also lose my hair after three or four months. But I thought it was more dangerous to keep getting fat than to have the surgery. I had accepted that I could not control my weight, and I accepted the fact that there was something I could do about it, and I did it. Acceptance is the solution to my problems; I accept my obesity, but I am not resigned to it. I accept the responsibility to change myself. I had the surgery three days ago.

Lola accepted that she had a weight problem and she believed that being overweight was an unacceptable way for her to live. It was through accepting her obesity as a problem that she set forth on a mission to change. It has been six months since her surgery, and she is happy with her choice.

Intimate Connection with Others

Interested and concerned about own life
and the lives of others,
from a practical and nonjudgmental perspective

Small network of close friends
who know and respect one another's deepest nature

Treats others with respect, holding individuals
in high esteem,
with a willingness to defer

Evokes the thoughts and feelings of others

Empathy and acceptance of the experiences
and feelings of others

25

Intimate connection is an elusive term meaning a link or communication between people. Noted relationship researcher John Gottman, Ph.D., reports that the single biggest determiner of a successful relationship is a sense of connection. But not all connections between people are healthy or positive. The ingredient that sets apart healthy and unhealthy connections is respect. Respect is the willingness to hold another in high regard, with a willingness to defer. The ways we show respect in our behavior and conversation are the same five qualities that we most admire in other people:

1. Courage
2. Kindness
3. Humor
4. Serenity
5. Altruism

It is through expressing these qualities in our words and behavior that we establish intimate healthy connections with others. Being intentional in our thinking allows us to claim and express the qualities within ourselves that we most admire.

We show *courage* by being receptive to the thoughts and beliefs of others, even when we don't agree, by simply acknowledging the merit of someone else's judgment, opinions, or wishes. We are courageous when we manage our fear, not allowing our differences to scare us away from one another.

Kindness is showing courtesy and care for others. It is going a little out of our own space to offer a gesture of compassion or generosity. Sometimes it's only a brief moment—a gentle smile or a softly spoken compliment—that expresses kindness.

Humor is seeing something as funny and responding with a laugh or smile. It is a way of affirming ourselves and others, showing that we are not in fear or anger, but that we feel safe and relaxed, accepting the relationship as joyful. It aids our relationships by preventing us from taking ourselves too seriously, and often it communicates that we do not have to have our own way and that we are flexible. Humor is healthy only when *everyone* is laughing; it is not funny if someone is hurt or offended.

Serenity is calmness and a state of confident acceptance. It means being at peace within oneself. Serenity allows intimacy to flourish between people because of the openness and spontaneity that is possible when there is no worry, shame, or anxiety.

Altruism is an interest in the welfare of others without personal gain. Being altruistic means being attentive to the needs of others and finding solutions to problems in a practical, logical style.

We possess all of these qualities, and by being deliberate in our thinking we can choose to live our lives with the ultimate self-respect and intimate connection with others.

"As human beings, our greatness lies not so much in remaking the world as in remaking ourselves." –Mahatma Gandhi

Intimacy is a close, familiar, personal relationship with another person that is usually affectionate. Intimacy requires trust, compassion, kindness, courage, empathy, humor, and so on. We can make intimacy so complex that we lose it trying to achieve it. Sometimes we can get so caught up in how we are supposed to be in relationships that we can overlook simple ways of being intimate.

Susan, a founder of *Bounce*, co-led one of the first *Bounce* Circles. Women started talking about sex, and Susan, at age 58, shared that as she had gotten herself "in shape" through her body-building she had felt like decorating her body with lovely bras and panties. She talked about the enjoyment she and her husband shared around her new-found sexiness. Susan went on to comment that she and her husband have a scheduled Saturday afternoon "play date," a sexual playtime.

One woman muttered, "Yuk, schedule sex?" Susan laughed, "It isn't so much scheduled sex as it is looking forward to having fun together. And we do. We talk and laugh and fool around. Sometimes we play "dress up" and occasionally we use sex toys. Whatever we end up doing we have fun. The discussion of Susan's "play dates" ended only because of the close of the evening.

Janet, who was a member of that Circle later wrote these comments. *I am a 46-year-old woman who has been married to the same man (Steve, 69 years old) for 25 years. While the love and respect was still very strong, the sizzle just wasn't there. I was lying in bed the Saturday following the first* **Bounce Circle** *meeting and decided that now was as good a time as any to explain Susan's concept to Steve. Now before I go further I must explain that Steve has always been very skeptical of "women's" groups.*

By the time I finished explaining Susan's concept of investing two to four hours a week in your relationship and that it would mean that he would come into town every Wednesday and we would meet at 4:00 to explore jazzing up our relationship, he had a whole new opinion of "women's" groups. I am confident that Susan has saved me from ever hearing a derogatory word about "women's" groups again. Hurray, Susan!

We have continued our weekly "meetings" (because they are *meetings and if you don't schedule them and give them the same weight you would a business conference, it won't work!). Steve shows up with champagne, treats, and always something imaginative. Myself, I have been to Lover's Package several times and find that I am emboldened by the passion that has been reignited in our relationship.*

Thank you, **Bounce!**

Janet's *Bounce* changed her life and her husband's life in a matter of weeks. The changes she made were fun and easy. It surprised her that he was so willing, and it is often true that men wait for women to take the lead in changing their relationship.

Couples who play together stay together

Enjoyment of Daily Life

Seeks joy daily

Revels in the ordinary

Celebrates the success of others

Lives in the moment

Appreciates self and others every day

It is vain to say human beings ought to be satisfied with tranquility: they must have action; and they will make it if they cannot find it.
– Charlotte Brontë

Living in the Moment

Seeking joy is a primary tenet of *Bounce* as well as a quality expressed by people who are happy and live at the 90%+ level of being their best. I believe that we find what we are looking for and if we look for joy we find it. Even in the hardest times, when life has dealt us pain and disappointment, seeking joy is an everyday choice anyone can make.

I am sharing a story that Sarah wrote about seeking joy. Sarah met her husband when they were both 17. They each attended college and studied accounting. Sarah and her husband had a son, Michael. Michael was born with a heart block that meant multiple surgeries, but few limitations in his life as he grew older.

Sarah had stopped working to be home with Michael, and her husband had become very successful. Knowing their marriage was strained, she was still shocked and wounded when he insisted on a divorce. It was not until a year after their divorce that he told her the truth. He had a one-year-old son with his former secretary. Of course Sarah felt devastated and betrayed, but instead of being angry or defensive, Sarah bounced.

Sarah, a gifted writer, wrote this story of a brief encounter with a man whose name she never knew. I am including it here as an example of transcending grief and disappointment to find joy in daily life and an appreciation of others. Being fully present in the moment, even when dreams don't come true.

Marathon Man of My Dreams

We jogged towards the general exhibition area, following the few participants we could see on the quiet, deserted streets. A man who had just gotten out of a white Volvo joined us, running behind and sometimes alongside my friend and I for what turned out to be six long blocks to 5th Avenue and Harrison. I was bubbly with endorphins and excitement. My friend was irritable and grouchy, so I found myself sharing my enthusiasm with this man.

I asked him if he was from here. He said the Eastside. Redmond. I told him I was from the Eastside, also. Bellevue. I asked him if he was running the half or full marathon. The man told me he would've run the full, but he was recovering from an injury. I told him this was my second race. I'd run the Vancouver half. A freezing wind hit my face. The man mentioned that he had signed up last night, because the weather had been so great. The previous day dawned blue skies and warm sun. I told him there was still a chance—that I was an optimist. He smiled.

At the check-in table, the man and I both fumbled, with tight fingers, taking off our gloves, picking up safety pins, and pinning our numbers to our jackets, with only two minutes until the start gun. Glancing over, I noticed he was not wearing a wedding ring as he pinned his number on his jacket. Pinning my number on, I thought how nicely my fingernails looked; manicured for a black-tie benefit I'd attended the previous night. I wondered if he noticed that I had no ring on, either.

"Does that hat keep you warm?" he asked. "I don't know," I told him, "I just bought it yesterday. I've never worn one before."

With all my hair stuffed inside, I was not feeling at all at my best, as contrasted with last evening's radiance: my hair styled, wearing a tight-fitting black satin dress and elegant evening pumps. The event was my first "coming out," since my marital breakup.

The moment we finished putting our gloves back on, we looked at each other. Then the man did something quite wonderful. He reached out his gloved hand for mine. I put my gloved hand in his and we squeezed tightly. I smiled up into his handsome face. "Good luck," I said. He smiled. I watched the man disappear into the crowd, as I ran off to join my friend.

Thousands of runners patted their hands and jumped in place at the start line, awaiting the start gun. Thirty seconds later the gun sounded. I took off running alongside my friend.

As it turned out, the rain stopped and the majority of the race was clear blue sky, no rain, and comfortable until the end when it grew blustery and cold again.

At the end of the race I was elated, while at the same time emotional. Back at the car, the white Volvo was gone. I'd connected in a major way with a man I might never see again, and he with me. There was a synergy to his gesture, a meaningful moment, which struck me as though he was trying to communicate that I was a pretty woman and worthy of being touched. Was I so hungry for touch that his gesture took on special meaning? My 27-year marriage ended, unexpectedly, just a year ago.

First thing Monday morning, I phoned my mentor friend to meet me for coffee. I call her my Nymph of Wisdom, an inspirational woman whose beauty, creativity, strength, insight, and independence I greatly admire. She has written several books on relationships, and she seems all-knowing about love and life.

With her sensuous black hair wrapped around her shoulder, her warm eyes engaged, and her body leaning towards me to listen, I asked her, "What is this feeling I'm feeling?"

"Emotional connection," she said.

"Is it real?" I asked.

"Of course," she said.

I smiled. I wriggled in my seat at the café.

"Not emotional dependence?" I asked her.

"No. He wanted to connect with you, too."

"I think that man did want something emotional from me," I said. "Even if it was just in that moment—it felt like a very intimate moment between us. It's a shame I'll never see him again."

"You can find him if you want to," she said.

"I can't," I moaned. "I can't possibly track him down. I didn't get his marathon number."

"Yes, you can. You saw his number."

"I did?"

"Yes. It's somewhere in your memory."

"It is?"

"If you want to remember the number, it will come back to you."

As I walked out of the café and to my car, I thought, I don't want to push these feelings away—I want to embrace them because they feel real. But what if he's married? What if he's a narcissist? I've chosen narcissistic men before: men who mask their inward self-absorption with their external charm, blind to beauty beyond themselves. I know what that feels like.

At home on my computer, I searched the participants' names listed on the marathon website. No addresses were available. Later that day, I called the organization committee and got a curt answer from a woman who said they did not give out participants' information. A few days later, when I received the published results in the official marathon catalogue, I underlined all the men's names listed in Redmond in the man's potential age group. More than 250 possibilities; how would I get in touch? Write? Get their phone numbers from directory assistance and call them? What would I say?

I looked up my name in the catalogue. Half Marathon Run: Female by Age. Female 45-49. 103 (out of 300) Sarah Williamson Bellevue WA 2:11:41. I ran 13.2 miles in 2 hours 11 minutes and 41 seconds. Not bad, I thought. Maybe he would remember my number and look me up. I closed my eyes, trying to recall his tag

Feeling distressed, I e-mailed a close friend.

.

"I ran in the half-marathon on Sunday, and I think I met the man of my dreams. Only one problem. I didn't get his tag number—so there's a good chance I will never see him again." She e-mailed me back.

"Can't believe you let a good man get away . . ."

I couldn't sleep, thinking about this man. I tossed and turned, then finally fell into a deep sleep. I dreamt. In my dream, marathon men are running everywhere, beautiful, fit men. Their body parts enlarge to enormous sizes, then the moment I reach out to touch them, they shrink to nothingness.

As I try to sleep, I reach out my arms to express my sensuality, my love, my warmth, my passion, my caring, my desire to touch and be touched. As the men come close, I run away, screaming "You obsessed, narcissistic men. You cannot see my beauty, only your own."

The next morning, without much sleep, I reflected on how my dream seemed fraught with fantasy and fear. I wondered: Should I continue to pursue this man, or leave him as the man of my dreams?

At week's end, I am in San Diego, California, on business. I run the quiet, deserted beach along the La Jolla Pacific Coast early one morning. I have on tight leggings and a running top that shows off my fitness. My dark Maui-Jim glasses hide my stare. Or so I think. My turned head gives me away. The marathon man of my dreams manifests into the surfer man of my dreams. The attractive, fit man hoisting a surfboard on his shoulder makes a groaning noise. The man, somewhere in his late 30s, is tall, tan, and gorgeous with long, wavy blond hair. He knows that I like what I see. I have no time to react. Not a smile. Not a gesture. Nothing. I continue my pace down the long, long stretch of sand. When I get to the rocky passage I must climb, I mount several boulders and turn, allowing myself a look back at the surfer from a distance. I feel like the French Lieutenant's Woman, mysterious and intriguing. I question myself: Does he like what he sees?

Back at the resort I look at myself in the mirror to see what the surfer might have seen. I am slender and fit with a symmetrically proportioned body. I have large, brown eyes, smooth clear skin, and glossy light brown hair to my shoulder. I smile. I have straight, white, teeth. And what's inside? I say out loud: a warm, generous heart.

There was a time when the only thing I could see in a man's reflection was his narcissism. Now, I'm in charge of my own sensuality. A gorgeous man is appreciating my beauty, and I like what I see, too.

I run back outside to the deserted beach in the direction of the surfer. I lift my arms high up in the air. I run as fast I can. Thank you I say out loud in tears running along the beach. Thank you to all you beautiful men for acknowledging me. A beauty I have never allowed myself to acknowledge. In the reflection of your beauty, I see my own, now. I can choose to regret that I may never see you again, or I can choose to love the feeling for what it is: a real moment of joy. Reality is rarely as good as the dream. The dream, left untouched, stays more pure. Thank you, thank you, thank you, I say out loud, to all you marathon men of my dreams for pure moments of joy. And that is enough.

Lives Altruistic Values

Focuses on the problems of others, searching for practical solutions without concern for personal gain

Lives with humility and transcends struggles through self-transformation

Accepts and respects the beliefs and values of others

Works for the greater good

37

Altruism is going beyond self for the well-being of others. It means giving—expecting nothing in return. Altruism can be heroic and on a grand scale, like the altruism the world has experienced from Bill and Melinda Gates. Or Oprah Winfrey, who has transcended and transformed herself throughout her life to become an inspiration to both men and women throughout the world. Altruism can also be a simple act of kindness, like allowing someone to go ahead of you in the grocery store line. Or donating time to a cause you care about.

The first story I'll tell to describe altruism is about my husband, Lynn. As I read the list of qualities we created to define altruism, I found myself thinking about him. He had a long career in medicine as a children's orthopedist (bone and joint doctor). He retired from surgery at 65, but continued teaching and writing textbooks.

After the 9-11-01 terrorist attacks, Lynn felt he should do something to make a difference, and being the very practical person that he is, he decided to do something he already knew how to do—create and write books.

He created an organization named Global-HELP.org. HELP is an acronym for <u>H</u>ealth <u>E</u>ducation <u>L</u>ow-cost <u>P</u>ublications. He now works full-time on HELP. He receives no salary or any compensation, in fact he donates money as well as time, energy, and thought. In the time Global-HELP has existed, he has overseen the production of about 60 different books that are available to health care workers throughout the world, free of charge.

One book in particular has had an impact of enormous proportion. He created, wrote, and published a book describing the treatment of clubfeet in children. Over 100,000 children are born each year with clubfoot and until recently many received little or no treatment, leaving some disabled or disowned. Lynn named the book for the person who developed a casting method for correcting the feet: Dr. Ignacio Ponseti. This little booklet has now been published in 13 different languages, 25,000 hard copies have been distributed worldwide, and over 200,000 have been downloaded from the Internet.

Lynn believes that we create world peace by equalizing world resources, and he lives what he believes. He is both modest and humble and he passionately works toward the greater good. That is not to say he is singularly focused, he is not. He is an excellent boater, small aircraft pilot, photographer, and visionary. Lynn is also a generous and loving husband, father and grandfather.

It is always best to build on our stengths and do what we know how to do. Sometimes seemingly incidental gestures make a difference in the lives of others. We all have skills and abilities that we can offer for the benefit of others.

Another story that illustrates living altruistic values is Patricia's. Patricia was broadsided when her husband announced he wanted a divorce. He was in love with someone else, he explained unapologetically, as though he expected Patricia to understand. The woman he was in love with had come to work with him so Patricia wouldn't need to work the weekends anymore. At least that was what he reasoned.

Patricia had been working her full-time job during the week and working with him in his business on the weekends. They had taken out loans to start the business—his dream—loans that she had signed. But at the moment of his announcement about a divorce, she wasn't thinking about that. Her head was spinning, looking for signs and signals that maybe she should have seen that he was involved with someone else. Looking back there were a few puzzling situations, but nothing glaring. Still, he pursued the divorce, and after nine months they reached a settlement.

She had the stable income, so she ended up paying him alimony and assuming responsibility for the business loans if he was unable to pay them. Her husband and his new love moved in together. What happened next is what usually happens with fiery, hot, new love—it burned out. Now the lovers who couldn't stand to be apart, couldn't stand to be together.

This was bad news for Patricia. Since the new lovers were battling, the business was failing and unable to pay its debts. She had a choice, pay the debts or ?. She paid. Of course, now her former husband wanted to come back, but once burned was enough for Patricia, especially after he admitted to other affairs.

Patricia was sad, angry, depressed and disillusioned until she decided she had enough of feeling bad. "Get over it she told herself," but nothing happened. Sometimes the best way to get over something is to get over *yourself*, and that is what she did. She lost her anger, disappointment and resentment and got compassion. She decided to do the Susan G. Komen Breast Cancer 3-Day®. Participants walk 60 miles in three days and help raise money for breast cancer support and research.

She started training in June, and each weekend, Saturday and Sunday, all summer long Patricia walked. Now Patricia is not a morning person, she admits, but every weekend morning she was up, putting on her shoes, and walking. By summer's end, she had walked 600 miles.

"Finishing the 3-Day® was one of the hardest things I have ever done, and one of the most rewarding," Patricia says. Patricia hasn't had breast cancer nor have any friends or family members. She did it simply for the well-being of others; that is altruism. An ability we all possess.

Transition to Transformation

Living life with joy, purpose and a positive sense of well-being gives us the ability to bounce. When we hit something hard, we energetically spring away, ready to face life with renewed energy and a new confidence in being better than ever. It is through this journey that we can transcend who we have been to be transformed into all we can be.

Life is full of surprises—the love we thought would last forever ends, or the career that we spent years developing takes a dive. Instead of developing our plans in a tidy and orderly fashion, we find all kinds of surprises—some filled with delight and wonder, like the birth of a child or the gift of friendship. Others, ill health or an untimely death, seem to threaten everything we know and believe about ourselves. Life has hard spots that we are not prepared for. Sometimes they are brief, other times they seem to linger far too long, but they do come and they continue to come throughout life, often without warning. It is these unexpected and unwanted experiences that push us to be more than we have been before.

It is through our natural desire to seek and learn that we transform over and over.

It is through this natural desire to explore that we can be transformed, changing from one way of being to another. And at each transformation we begin to prepare for the next. Some transformations are easy and they seem to just happen. Others are filled with turmoil and upset. One thing for sure, they keep coming. We can embrace them or resist them, but they are a natural and inevitable part of our lives.

Transformations with **Bounce** mean going beyond better, far beyond to a new way of being. **Bounce** only requires the willingness to explore the unknown, the untried, and untested. You may feel awkward and unsure. Sometimes nothing seems right, nothing is familiar, then you try something else, and *bingo!* It works. Growth comes from the courage to continue the journey even when you don't know where you are going. Sometimes you just have to be where you are. It is during these times of uncertainty that we are transformed.

"Two little boys, fascinated by a butterfly trying to struggle out of its chrysalis decided that the butterfly needed some help. Approaching the struggling insect carefully, they slit the chrysalis, helping the butterfly to make an immediate exit. The butterfly staggered with its damp wings plastered next to its body and then after resting quietly for a few moments, died. Horrified, the boys rushed to their father who then explained about the butterfly and struggle. He told them that the butterfly needed to struggle to leave the chrysalis, as this process pumps the blood through its wings so that it can emerge and fly. Struggle is often that which makes us stronger and able to survive." –Gayle Duncan

Transformation is Changing from One Way of Being to Another

"Human life will never be understood unless its highest aspirations are taken into account. Growth, self-actualization, the striving toward health, the quest for identity and autonomy, the yearning for excellence (and other ways of phrasing the striving "upward") must by now be accepted beyond question as a widespread and perhaps universal human tendency." –Abraham Maslow, Ph.D.

Ann's Story

Ann's story begins at childhood. She had deadly allergies and asthma at a time when medicine had little to offer. As a young girl she lived a sheltered and protected life—a lifestyle necessary for her survival. She missed years of school, but did not think of herself as different or left out.

During early adulthood her sheltered upbringing left her naive in choosing a husband. Even as she was dating her future husband, she had concerns about his temper, but she kept those concerns to herself. Ann bounced through her childhood illness and went into a quiet adulthood then into motherhood. At middle age she was becoming more isolated and more frightened, until she decided it was time to take her life into her own hands for the first time, at age 60. Her transition was courageous and her transformation profound. This is Ann's story.

As I was growing up, I rarely felt that I was different from anyone else, but in actuality my upbringing was quite different because of health issues. I was born in January of 1933 and I have a sister four years older. We lived comfortably north of Seattle, and our family was very close, including grandparents, aunts, uncles and cousins.

When I was a few months old, my mother added egg to my bottle formula, as this was done in those days for extra nutrition. I immediately had an allergic reaction, and to this day, nuts and eggs cause me to have an anaphylactic response.

As time went on, I developed eczema and asthma, the latter being triggered by childhood colds. Consequently my education was interrupted for long periods of time each year, and I was withheld entirely from attending the fifth grade. It was not until the middle of the eighth grade that my doctor felt I could handle the exposure to classroom colds. During those years, I was tutored when I was not in the oxygen tent or recuperating, so my education consisted of the basic three Rs, at best. At the same time my eczema was at its worst, so my beloved piano lessons were hit and miss.

Wheezing and struggling to breathe was exhausting, monotonous, and boring, but I never was concerned that anything might happen to me. I just accepted this malady and knew I would some day get better.

I dearly missed associating with my school friends and playing the usual neighborhood games of hide and seek, bike riding, etc. but I did what I could, when I could. Going to summer camp and overnights at friends were out of the question because of my food allergies and a chance of a sudden spell of asthma. Even though I could not participate in these normal activities, I still never thought of myself as being different. I credit my parents for this feeling. It never occurred to me that my friends might think of me as being sick.

Eczema is painful. Coughing and moving around made it worse. In an attempt to keep Ann quiet and make breathing easier for her she spent a lot of time in a green oxygen tent.

Ann had a happy childhood and although she couldn't always participate in the same activities as other kids, she never thought of herself as being different.

Ann's parents made every effort to allow her to be with other children when her health permitted it. This was a birthday party for her, but some birthdays she could not be around other kids if the flu was going around.

These years were very difficult for my sister, as her activities were curtailed since many family activities were designed around me. I never remember hearing a complaint from her even when the family took me to an allergy specialist in Philadelphia. This month-long trip in 1943 took her out of school during her freshman year of high school. To this day, I credit the strong family love and respect for one another for a part of my healing.

There was one particular time, I later realized, that my parents thought they might lose me, but this was never discussed. It was my mother who was always there to give me that shot of adrenalin when needed. This time my father gave me the shot and sat by my side holding my hand.

Since I spent many weeks and months at home, I learned to enjoy the many crafts and quiet activities that my parents made available to me. Consequently, to this day I am just as content pursuing my own interests as functioning in a group. During my years at home between these bouts of asthma and eczema, I led as normal a life as possible. Because of my reclusive lifestyle, it became harder and harder for me to step into the mainstream with my peers. When possible, my mother would arrange for me to attend an art class or event at school, and it took extra courage to suddenly present myself, especially in middle school. I remember with pleasure the little moments when the curtain around the oxygen tent would be moved aside—that meant I didn't need as much oxygen and I was getting better.

I still cherish and enjoy simple pleasures, as I take time to notice the beauty of the garden, the ever-changing lake, and the morning sunrises.

I never wanted to be different from others or stand out. Obviously I was very naive. I learned not to let a disability consume or control my life any more than necessary and to develop interests outside.

Looking back over my illness, I feel I learned that the mind can play a very major role in the healing process. The nurturing and love given by family and friends and a very capable and caring physician had a very positive role. All of this taught me about building and strengthening of my ability to face new and monumental problems, and to always be thankful for the present, as my situation was not unique from many others.

These lessons paved the way for me to cope with and work through different kinds of challenges I had to face in later years. I feel it gave me an inner strength to deal with situations out of my control, but this was also obtained through the help of others. Childhood illness left me socially and emotionally innocent and trusting.

During an asthma attack at college, I called my mother to take me home. While I was waiting, the house mother, a Christian Scientist, spoke with me in a comforting voice about the beauty of the trees that time of year, and as we talked my wheezing stopped. By the time my mother arrived, the attack was over. That lesson has helped me many times. When I have had an allergic reaction and needed to get to the hospital immediately, I said to myself, "Don't worry, we will get there in time. Don't worry."

This may be why to this day I do not have fear when I am being rushed to the emergency room when a piece of nut accidentally falls into my food. I do not let my food limitations interfere with my social activities, as a missed meal is never a problem.

My real-life experience was very elementary, compared to my sorority house peers. The same held true for my education, as at this point I had only been out in the real world and attending school regularly for four and a half years. I felt very inadequate in the area of literature and writing, so I struggled through many courses. The entrance requirements at the University of Washington were not as demanding in my day as they are now. Through the years I was taught to stick with whatever you were doing, so this perseverance made up for some of my lack of early education.

After completing four years of college (I did not graduate), I was swept off my feet by a charming young man, and we were married less than a year after meeting each other. Twice when we were dating, I considered calling off the wedding. Each time he had become angry—too angry for the incident, but I was not worldly enough to recognize these quirks as real trouble ahead. I thought of telling my mother about my concern, but when she asked me if everything was OK I quietly said, "Yes," and she did not question my hesitation. So we went ahead with the wedding. When we returned from our honeymoon, my mother had destroyed all the photo albums that contained any pictures of me with past boyfriends. All of my pictures from high school and college days were gone. My new life was with my husband.

I never heard my mother criticize or seriously question my father. I thought they had a good marriage, and I would emulate them. My husband's bad temper and a controlling personality did not foster good parenting and a strong marriage. My illness plagued my childhood, and the way I was raised taught me to accept, not fight, my husband's actions. Most of the time, acceptance is a gift I am glad to possess, but at the time I married, a little more questioning and discussion would have been a good idea. I didn't know how to talk about problems or concerns or who to talk to.

Our life evolved into what I thought it should be. He worked at the bank, we had two children and a nice home, and under my father's encouragement he was promoted rapidly. I never challenged anything my husband did or said, as my upbringing taught me it was not appropriate to argue.

I was aware that my husband had some disagreeable relationships with my sister, her husband, and our cousins. I, of course, sided with my husband without question and my sister and I had limited contact for many years, except when we were helping our parents during their years of illness.

In all, I felt I had a very wonderful life at last. I was able to manage my allergies and asthma (thanks to new medicines). My job was to raise our two children and become involved in community activities. I loved caring for our children and being part of the community. I was a hostess for friends and business associates. I had grown up with the sense of civic and community interest and responsibility. My parents instilled their values in philanthropy and community service by example.

My mother cut patterns from five layers of fabric to be sewn for clothing for refugees during and after World War II. We put together boxes for service people. I supported the Children's Foundation at Everett General Hospital, volunteering and fundraising. I enjoyed my children and their friends and my husband and his colleagues.

I played tennis and golf, as well as bridge, with friends. I was active in several charities, especially those that cared for children. The middle years of our marriage were good. Our children were doing well in high school and beginning college. Our life was normal and routine. We had good times traveling together and with friends, but increasingly my husband fell apart if everything didn't go his way.

As time went on, my marriage was becoming more difficult. Looking back, the change was gradual. I would have never accepted some of my husband's behavior if it had started earlier in our marriage. Over the years, his comments became dismissive, critical and ill-mannered. Some of these characteristics I attributed to his childhood background, and others simply became normal in my mind.

My husband had always been very controlling, and he became more angry and abusive as the years went on. He controlled all of the money, even the money I inherited from my parents. I had bounced from my childhood illness, but I felt myself sinking under the pressure of his unpredictable attacks as they became more hostile and more physical. Other than our children, my family did not know about the abuse—pride and brain-washing kept me silent. I did not know who to talk to about these increasing problems. I felt ashamed, embarrassed, and alone.

47

Since I had married right out of college and had always been under the care of my parents or influence of my husband, I couldn't imagine what it would be like to be on my own. I started thinking about divorce in 1985 after a "small" beating. I went to an attorney, a friend of the family, who advised me to get counseling and to try harder to make my marriage work. Staying with him another eight years cost me more than time, as it also cost me my hearing. The repeated shaking and slapping permanently damaged my eardrum.

A few years before when I went to sign in at a board meeting and was told I had no stock, I began to ask questions about my money.

It had to be done. I had to get a divorce. It was the only right answer, but I hesitated again. Time passed and our relationship was usually "not too bad." The turning point was on a Mediterranean cruise with friends. Arriving at the airport I was thinking maybe I could excuse myself, but I boarded the plane with bruised hands and arms, and a very sore hip from where he had kicked me while I lay on the floor, covering my head and ears.

One beautiful night on the ship, I stood at the rail as we were leaving port. I questioned again whether I should leave; this time I decided I had to. We rented a car in Portugal and I was to navigate as he drove. When he thought I directed him the wrong way, he screamed at me and refused to stop for lunch or sights of interest. I had gotten extra cash on the ship and packed a sweater and slacks in a small tote, as I thought I might have to escape one of his outbursts of temper.

"*I felt alone and ashamed; his insults and hostility made me feel worthless and stupid.*"

I was further convinced I must take the big step upon returning home and strike out on my own for the first time ever. I mustered up my courage. I talked with both my adult children. With the blessing of my children, my sister, and cousins, I left. I knew I had to stay on course this time. It was always seductive to think things might get better, but I knew from years of experience that we always went back to the same pattern of seemingly normal behavior until the next explosion, and all the physical and emotional abuse would begin again. I had to forge ahead, and look to the future and end the marriage. I have always lived by a quote from one of my childhood tutors, "It is always darkest before the dawn." These were truly dark times.

My early experiences of being in and out of school and having to adjust in a world that I could not control because of my health limitations, gave me the courage to step out on my own. I didn't know what to expect or what I could or could not do, but I knew I had to leave, no matter what.

I tried to talk to him at our cottage with our kids present, but he became angry again. I went home, but he followed me. I heard the creak of his footsteps on stairs and ran out of the house and hid at the home of a friend. Bit by bit, I made my way. Finally I was free of him.

I no longer accept everything people tell me; now I insist on understanding. I have gained confidence and freedom, but it also hurts me deeply to know I have been betrayed by people I loved and trusted.

I learned from my childhood struggles to get professional help. I set up a support team, of my choosing, to advise and guide me through this quagmire and set the scene for this wonderful stage of life. I chose people whom I respect and who respect me. My freedom also brought some surprises.

I was overwhelmed by the love of old friends who stepped forward in support of my decision, many telling terrible stories of their dealings with my husband. I was shocked and embarrassed, but with guidance, love, and forgiveness of my sister and friends, I found new strength and abilities I never knew I possessed. I bounced, again. I began making my own way in the world and enjoying a new circle of friends. I also became aware of other relationships in my life that I now realized were not normal. It was the first time I felt I could be candid about problems and concerns, and talk to other people about them.

Teaching and nurturing two of my granddaughters is a wonderful part of my life. I found a college for one of them and helped them sort out complicated emotions about their parents and grandfather. I have been able to be an advocate for them and they have given me the opportunity to guide them. We appreciate and respect each other, the way I now know families should.

To this day, I am as grateful for the world about me as I was during my childhood days, especially those days when I was not wheezing and scratching. Unknowingly, these days uniquely prepared me for a bumpy future and allowed me to blossom beyond my imagination.

Whenever a project seemed so large that I did not know where to begin, I would tell myself to start nibbling. This holds true whether weeding a garden or chasing down lost figures in a ledger. My father used to tell me not to beat a dead horse, as I would keep trying to get something to work when it was definitely beyond repair. Knowing when to quit is important. Quit what doesn't work, and keep going. Leave the past behind.

The first two years after I fled from my home, I went back through 40 years of documents and records, tracing the money my parents had left me. Money that was supposed to be separate property had been moved into joint accounts and spent. Painstakingly I organized and tracked thousands of transactions. I met with accountants, attorneys, trust officers and bankers until I was able to understand what had happened and what was legal and what wasn't. It was a disturbing awakening to discover my own complicity in draining the family resources because I had been afraid to insist on knowing what was happening.

I have never enjoyed people like I do now. I feel so grateful to have so many interesting people in my life. I went to a luncheon last week with some of my college friends, and four of the women at the table were more concerned about how the tomato on their plate was sliced than about what was happening in the world. Then I realized I could have been like that if I hadn't gotten out of my marriage. I grew up in a box and then my husband kept me in a box. I wasn't allowed to go out with anyone without his permission. As awful as the divorce was, I am so glad I got out.

Now I make sure I understand everything that happens in my life, whether it is my money or my health—and if I don't, I keep asking until I do. I have created quite a team of advisors, but that is what it takes for me to know what's going on. It is money well spent as far as I am concerned.

My childhood tutor said, "It is always darkest before the dawn," but the important thing to remember is that there is always a dawn! My advice to you is to use your experiences throughout the years to savor every day of your life, even though it may not have taken you down the path of your dreams. There are so many hidden pleasures in the world, ranging from observing the first spring blossom to small successes of others. Find joy and **Bounce***: Go beyond your limitations—far beyond.*

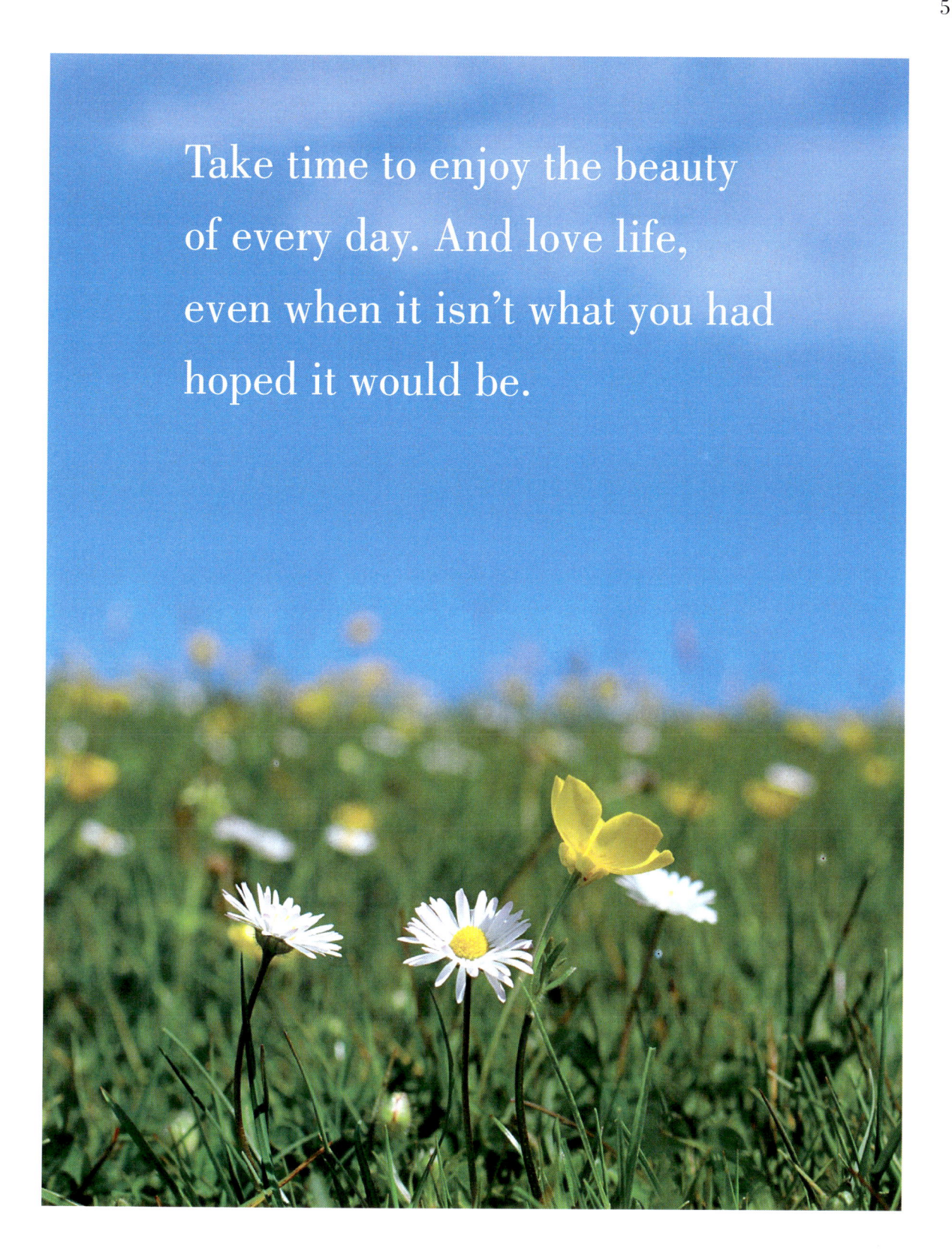

Take time to enjoy the beauty of every day. And love life, even when it isn't what you had hoped it would be.

TRANSITION

Transitions are the in-between spaces from what was to what will be. When we move away from the known into the unknown there is a kind of unfamiliar energy. For some it is a nervousness; others experience it as excitement; most agree it is uncomfortable. Transition precedes transformation and transformation cannot occur without transitions.

The first awareness of transition may be barely noticeable, like being bored with a once-interesting television show. Or as dramatic as "I just can't live like this anymore!" Usually there is a sense of desire driving us in a certain direction. Both feelings are murmurs of change to come.

Focusing on "things" is usually a detour; transitions are about internal not external changes. New stuff is just new stuff that interferes with the type of transitions that lead to transformation.

We all know people who collect cars, redecorate houses, change jobs, get new clothes, buy new equipment or have plastic surgery, but always seem dissatisfied. "Stuff" masks and interferes with meeting needs. Core needs are the source of our desire for change, but the only changes that meet our aesthetic needs are internal. It is the drive to be better as a person that meets the need for growth.

Transition—a process or period in which something undergoes a change and passes from one state, stage, form, or activity to another.

Transitions can include activities like a makeover to change appearance. Or it can involve learning a new skill or simply having a new experience. The uncertainty of transition accompanied by feelings from enthusiasm to apprehension can feel bumpy and disorganized. Many people describe it as nervousness. It is energy needed in the next stage of transformation. In the meantime, it is just there.

Women who have had children by natural birth will remember the transition stage of labor, the phase with the strongest uterine contractions just before giving birth. The transition from being a pregnant woman to having a real-live baby. Certainly an example of struggle before result.

A profound little book on transitions is Spencer Johnson's *Who Moved My Cheese?* It's the story of two mice who find their cheese has been moved. They have a choice: continue doing what they have always done or do something new! It is a story of transition and transformation.

Turning restlessness inward creates self-doubt that becomes anxiety. Allow yourself to feel both anxious and footloose; it's merely an awkward time. And it's not an indication that you are making a mistake. Remember the story of the two boys learning that the butterfly had to struggle and eat its way out of the chrysalis in order to transform into a butterfly? The same is true for us: Struggle is necessary for transition and transformation.

Early in the coaching process, I want to know about my client's fears because they are nearly always working toward making them come true. Here are a few examples:

Fear of being unlovable, made true by being unloving.

Fear of losing money, but taking risks in the stock market.

Fear of losing his family, made true by seldom being home and involved.

Women who fear their husband will leave them make it a sure thing by leaving sex at the bottom of the "to do" list. Every woman has a fear of becoming a bag lady and many make it come true by not paying attention and saving their own money.

The irony is that these dreaded fears are often the key to freedom and transformation if they are recognized and accepted. Sometimes the worst thing that can happen to you is the best thing for you, if you bounce.

We focused **Bounce** on women at age 50+ because it is such an important and new transition and transformation opportunity. It is the first time in our history when women who are invited to join AARP (American Association of Retired People) are so young in mind and body. While there are more women who will be eligible for retirement, retirement brings a number of problems with it.

Of course there are financial issues; most people will outlive their money. Most women who think they can retire at 65 will have to cut their cost of living by at least 30%, assuming they do have a substantial personal or corporate retirement plan. Counting on government aid in the form of Social Security seems like a high-risk bet. We have an enormous national debt to be paid by future generations. Looking forward, we have a smaller number of people working and paying taxes and a larger number of people drawing from tax dollars. Studies show that we deplete the actual money we paid into Social Security a few years after we stop working. It just doesn't make sense that we can be employed for 40 years and live off savings and social benefits for another 30 years. The math just doesn't work. But that is just one of the problems that comes with the idea of retirement.

There are several age calculators on the Internet, *realage.com* or *livingto100.com*, but a simple formula is that you can reasonably expect to live 20 years longer than your grandparents. I took the survey on both and by their predictions I could live to be 100. Personally, I am not sure I want to, but I might have to. My mother-in-law, who died at 101, always said she wanted to die at 90, then she changed it to 95, but at 100 she said, "You just can't die because you want to; your survival instincts just don't let you do that."

Depression and anxiety also come with retirement. No wonder, considering the core needs that are met through work—biological needs, like food and shelter; belonging needs, being part of a group of a daily basis; and self-esteem needs of recognition, appreciation, and respect. Health issues also become bigger with retirement, but one of the biggest factors in ill health is loneliness. It is easy to become isolated when you don't have to get up and go.

We are referring to work as meaningful activity, not employment. Work can be child-rearing, volunteering, gardening or homemaking. A good definition for work is a meaningful activity that involves a stretch, or going beyond what you know you can do, in a way that makes a difference—in someone else's life; caring for the planet; starting a business or learning a new skill. Successful work also includes contact with other people, maybe one of the most important criteria for **Bounce** women—connection with other women focused on growth and transformation.

Over the years I have found that one of the most difficult questions clients have had to answer is, *What do you want?* On the surface it seems simple, but it isn't. It is easiest to think about what we don't want or don't like—I don't want to be sick, I don't like my job, I don't like the way my husband . . . and so on.

The best way we have found to know what you really want is to think about core needs, and think about how they are or are not being met. Needs are requirements. They are essential to our survival and well-being. Unmet needs will nag at us, but met needs are pretty invisible.

Joyce, 55, had raised three kids and all were grown. She had worked full-time for 20 years after the kids went to school. She wanted to retire from her job as a realtor, she didn't really like selling real estate. Joyce and her husband, Hank, had talked about early retirement for years. Hank was a salesman, but didn't like his job. He had always wanted to do something else, but felt he had a responsibility to his family. Neither wanted to work.

Their home was valued at $300,000 in 2004 with a $50,000 mortgage. They had combined retirement accounts of $400,000, giving them $250,000 after-tax money from their home, and $400,000 in untaxed assets. They didn't want to work, they agreed. They were young enough to life and so that is what they were going to do.

Core needs met through work
- Biological needs—shelter, food, safety, security
- Belonging needs—being part of a work group or community
- Self-esteem needs—recognition, appreciation and respect

Joyce did not want to sell their house, she loved her home. They talked with a counselor who encouraged them to *live their dream.* Their financial advisor insisted they leave their money in the stock market. He advised, "If you don't leave your money in the market, you will be 65 years old and have to go back to work; $400,000 isn't enough to retire."

Joyce and Hank both quit their jobs and borrowed $2,000 a month against their home so they would have money to travel. They traveled to places they had always wanted to see. They went to Paris in the spring, then the Greek Isles, they took a cruise in the Caribbean and hiked in Glacier Park. The first two years were wonderful. It was the third year they started to worry. Housing prices and the market were down. By the fourth year they were scared.

By 2008, their home had dwindled in value and they had loans against their home for $150,000. Their stock portfolio was now valued at $250,000, leaving them with a decreased net worth of $300,000—not enough to retire on. Both now needed jobs, but the job market was tight. Houses weren't selling. They could not find work.

Getting what you want involves trade-offs, and nobody knows the future. Do an inventory of what you want, making sure that you are not exchanging needs for wants. Joyce and Hank's needs for food, safety and shelter; belonging needs; love needs; and self-esteem needs had been well-met, but four years later *all those needs were threatened.* Hank was depressed and had stopped even looking for a job. Joyce blamed herself, feeling she had pushed them into this.

The **Bounce** Circle helped Joyce review her needs and be intentional about how to meet her needs moving forward. We cannot change the past or the future, only the present. Reviewing her needs and being intentional about how to meet those needs helped Joyce **bounce.** Joyce realized that they had been so aware of what they didn't like, their jobs, they didn't think about changing themselves of their jobs, they just wanted out.

She decided to first meet with the bank and find out about lowering their mortgage payments. The bank recommended a debt consolidation program. She had to wait two weeks to get an appointment with a credit counselor, and she decided that might be a good job possibility for her. It was; she went to work for a nonprofit helping people restructure their debt. She loves being in the position of helping people, and she knows all too well how easily financial problems can spring up.

Joyce and Hank agreed he would get up with her in the morning and exercise, get showered and dressed for work, leave when she did, and not come back to the house until 5 p.m. It took about six months for him to put together two part-time jobs—one at a boutique grocery store and the other doing customer service at a bookstore.

Joyce says, This is not what we thought life would be like in our 60's but it is O.K. I like helping people and Hank likes working at the grocery store. He loves being part of the team, and he likes the bookstore because he gets to read all the techy stuff when they aren't busy. We don't really consider retirement anymore—maybe in our late 70s—and not just because of the money. We had been so focused on what we didn't want, we lost sight of our needs. We found that we get a lot out of being around people we like, and doing something useful. We *bounced* back, actually we bounced *beyond.*"

Stages of Transition

Bounce has four stages of transition that lead to transformation. *Consciousness* is the first. It is realizing that everything we think may not be true. Sometimes we have learned things that were never true, other times researchers have found a different answer, and sometimes what we think is obsolete. For instance, therapists used to tell people they had to fix what is wrong with them before they could become whole and happy. We now know that is not true. Whatever we think about—good or bad—happens.

Willingness to change is the second stage. Willingness is the readiness to rethink how you are living in the world and begin to form an idea of what direction you may want to go. This is not a plan with specific steps aimed at a specific outcome. It is a thought about how or what might be different about you or your experiences. This step is one that can be discouraging because of not being sure what you are doing. It is very uncomfortable for most of us if someone asks, "What's next for you?" and your only answer is "I don't really know." But that is the truth, and not knowing is part of growth. Acceptance is knowing change is coming and welcoming it.

There is no one right way to put it all together. It is your journey to create and enjoy.

Pruning is the third stage in transition. Pruning means clearing out the old to make room for the new. Growth cannot happen unless there is time, space, and energy for it to occur. Feelings of sadness and loss are part of transition. Even though it is time to move on, it is important to safeguard the pleasures of the past in your memory and not minimize them to justify letting them go.

Pleasure and passion is the fourth stage. This is an exciting time when the journey seems to have taken you someplace new and amazing. This is the WOW! New relationships, new surroundings, new skills. Some people call this the honeymoon stage, and it does have similarities. Everything is full of hope and promise with dreams to be explored and realized. The body even helps, pumping high levels of adrenaline-like chemicals through your brain. It is in truth a real natural high. Life is exciting, full of joy and meaning, and you feel like the best you have ever been—and you are.

Four stages of transition
Consciousness
Willingness
Pruning
Pleasure and passion

The transition has become a transformation when the new becomes part of who you are. The caterpillar becomes the butterfly, the tadpole a frog, and you are new. When one way of being is exchanged for another, the transformation is complete.

Consciousness—Don't Believe Everything You Think

It is not only our own beliefs that can become tethers in our lives, expert guidance also changes us. Beliefs affect our lives in big and small ways. I grew up thinking water drains the opposite direction in the Southern Hemisphere than in the Northern Hemisphere because of the earth's rotational pull. It isn't true. The way water drains depends mostly on the sink, no matter if it is north or south of the equator. Believing water flows one way or another in the tap does not have much impact on my day-to-day life, so unless I am playing a trivia game it doesn't really matter.

Other beliefs do affect day-to-day life. Drinking eight glasses of water a day has been the gospel for good health, leading many people to carry water bottles everywhere. Drinking eight glasses of water each day does not affect weight loss, change the hydration of cells, or help the mind or body stay young. Research now shows that we drink when we are thirsty and there is no specific right amount. And, in fact, drinking too much water is actually harmful.

It is more important to manage our thoughts and attitudes about what happens to us than the seriousness or trauma of the experience itself.

Many counselors have believed that understanding your childhood—the rejections, losses, and disappointments—is necessary to becoming a fully functional adult. Recent studies have shown that recalling the past and talking about it creates a focus that is usually negative. The more we think about something, the larger the neural pathways in the brain become. Remember, an interneural pathway is like a foot path; the more it is used, the bigger it gets. The same is true for thoughts. The more we think about the past, the more important the past becomes.

Doctors used to believe that sexual abuse during childhood meant that as an adult the person's sexual desires and behavior would be abnormal. Not true, recent studies say. Nearly a third of girls and 15% of boys have inappropriate sexual contact during childhood, usually with someone the family knows. Most of these children grow into healthy, normal, sexual adults who believe the molestation "was just something that happened." The exception is people who think of themselves as victims. Victims tend to continue to be victims. It is more a matter of how we think about what happens to us than what actually happens.

Do you believe . . .

some people are just born happy?

Yes, it is true. Around 2 or 3 percent of people are hyperthymic or happy all the time.

the death of a parent or divorce during childhood leaves permanent emotional scars?

False. Recent studies report that childhood trauma only adversely affects people who believe that it does.

keeping a journal of negative emotional experiences helps let go of them?

False. Thinking negative thoughts, writing about negative experiences, and repeatedly telling others of negative experiences creates more negative feelings.

shaving makes hair grow back faster, darker, and coarser?

False.

reading in dim light damages vision?

False.

wearing your hat will prevent you from catching a cold?

Viruses and bacteria don't care if you are cold. If anything, they prefer warmth.

you shouldn't go swimming after eating?

False. There is no time delay required for swimming.

thinking positive thoughts averts depression?

False. Clinical depression involves complex chemical interactions and usually precludes believing positive thoughts.

if you visualize yourself with the symbols of success, you will be successful?

False. Imagining yourself with money, jewelry, accolades or other symbols of success is unrelated to real-life success, although visualizing the steps you could take toward success is useful.

when you are feeling bad, you should think about how fortunate you are compared to others?

False. Thinking of the suffering of others does not make anyone feel better. When you are already feeling bad, you just feel guilty, believing you have little cause for your feelings considering how fortunate you are. Doing a good dead for others does help.

Willingness to change, the second stage of transition, means intentionally choosing to be different than you have been before. Of course you cannot know precisely how you will be different, but you do know you will experience, learn, grow, and transform. The other option—not changing—leads to deterioration. We can look to the body for evidence. We either exercise our muscles or they become weak. Waiting for change to happen to us is risky—the longer you wait, the more difficult change becomes. Human beings do not have a "hold" button. We can only go forward or backward, and having a sense of control over our lives is the single most important element in being happy.

The willingness to change and embark on a journey toward transformation seems scary at times, but it is the resistance to change that creates stress and, worse yet, distress. There is struggle in transition—at times leading to feelings of uncertainty, confusion, stress or fright, but it is a natural process that will run its course if you stick with it. Thinking of change as an adventure, a new experience, or a normal part of life allows us to glide through our transitions. It is through our willingness to learn and discover that we evolve into being our best. Embrace change and go willingly into the transformation process, seeking joy, welcoming new experiences, and discovering the best you.

It is through our willingness to learn and discover that we evolve into being our best.

Sharon loved being a homemaker. Her three children ranged in age from 2–17 years. Her husband, Brad, worked long hours in a start-up biotech company. This was his second start-up business; the first was sold to an international conglomerate, making Brad and Sharon a substantial amount of money. They lived in an upscale neighborhood with all the trimmings, beautiful home, private schools for their children, sports cars and SUVs, new cars for the boys when they turned 16, designer clothes, everything and anything they wanted. Brad and Sharon never argued. Their home was quiet and peaceful.

Brad initiated counseling. He was tired of his life; he wanted something more. "I've worked my tail off the past 25 years so you and the kids could have it all," he told Sharon. "Now I need time for Brad." Brad wanted a separation. He agreed to take six months to reconsider, but didn't really make much effort. Sharon was devastated, but unlike many women in her situation, she said, "I didn't expect this, but I have to change. My life will have to go in a different direction than I expected." Brad assured her that she would always be taken care of financially, and he would always take care of and be there for her and the kids, but he wanted a divorce.

Sharon relied on her spirituality to guide her. While she is not religious, she is someone with a strong sense of humanistic values, believing in kindness, generosity, and self-fulfillment. She went through all the grieving emotions: shock, fear, anger, guilt, sadness, and then acceptance.

When she was in shock, she focused on her own feelings, not asking Brad to justify his decision to leave. When she felt angry, she focused on her own sadness and disappointment, not blaming Brad. When guilt surfaced, she forgave herself. And when she came to the acceptance stage, she credited herself with her transformation. Throughout the process she kept her focus on herself. She started exercising daily, learned yoga, began meditating, and joined a book group. She volunteered at a food bank and decided to learn Spanish.

Sharon walked into the transition with her personal values in the forefront, and she stuck to them! Her transition, then transformation, was elegant and two years after the divorce, she was fit, happy, connected to a wonderful group of friends, giving back to her community, and she is in love. But that's not the end of the story. Brad quit his job to have time for himself. He did some traveling, did some reading, played tennis, and hung out, but by the time he was ready to go back to work, he found the world around him changed and his reputation had been damaged. He had not worked for three years and he stopped paying Sharon the money he promised.

What did Sharon do? She bounced again. She sold her house, moved to a less expensive neighborhood, and launched her own business. More than once she was tempted to hurt him back by withholding the kids or telling them the changes they had to make were his fault, but she didn't. Being practical and committed to her values, she asked him for the help he is able to offer—childcare.

Sharon says, "This is not what I wanted my life to be. I wanted to stay home with my kids. But this is my life and I love my kids and my friends. I have great health and I care about Brad. I feel compassion for him. He is a good man and the father of my children. I hope he finds what he is looking for. I have.

"I have a confidence in myself I would not have had. My kids have learned that life isn't perfect. When the chips are down, we all pitch in and do what needs to be done. We are closer as a family than before. I am healthier and more self confidant than I could have imagined. And, my sons and daughter have a more realistic view of life, and I am glad for that. All in all we are better off than we were. I wish we could have handled our problems differently and stayed together as a family, but we are still a family, really. We are kind and loving with each other, and I am glad for that, too."

PRUNING

It takes room to Bounce, and since most of our lives are full, we have to make room for something new. I call it pruning, removing some parts of life so that other parts can grow. Although I knew that I would like to write another book and pass on all I have learned from my clients over the years, I found it difficult to let go of what I had. I have a delightful group of clients, a wonderful husband, enough money, a loving and generous group of friends, opportunity to travel and so on. But, as Maslow suggested, the drive to do what we are capable of doing was pushing me out of my comfortable and enjoyable life. I needed something new, challenging, exciting, and a little bit scary.

Pruning is cutting branches away from a plant to encourage fuller growth

It was difficult. I had pruned my life before. It is the same as caring for a garden; parts have to be cut away so there can be new growth. I have seen a number of people try to get around pruning, not wanting to "cut out anything." I knew that wouldn't work for me and I also knew nothing has to be forever. If I removed something now and it wasn't right, I would do it over until it was right. I started by simply not taking new clients.

One of the most difficult and important areas to prune is relationships. Countless hours and bundles of time and energy get spent on relationships that don't work. The more difficult relationships can be those that aren't too bad. Relationships that aren't disastrous or abusive can go on and on without ever being rewarding or healthy. Sometimes both people keep trying because they think it should work or because they want to change each other, for the better, of course—and that never works. Carol and Chris are a great example of a relationship that needed pruning.

Carol and her sister, Chris, three years younger, were always at odds, even as little girls. Chris was a high-drama girl; tears and tantrums if she didn't like her dinner or her dress. Carol was easy-going, full of humor, and careful. Chris made messes and Carol cleaned them up. Chris screamed and Carol soothed.

When their parents divorced, Chris went with her father, on her insistence, while Carol preferred to stay with her mother. Chris thought her mother was stupid and her father brilliant. As they grew older, the sisters spent little time together—mostly because Carol felt that every occasion became a three-ring circus, with Chris the sole performer, ending in a tirade against Carol.

They were both in their 40s when their mother suffered a "nervous breakdown." She imagined she was an agent for the CIA and was being sent to the hospital as part of an undercover operation. Chris had lived about 75 miles from her mother for the past 10 years. She visited her mother and Carol once a year usually, an experience that never seemed to go well.

When Carol called Chris to tell her about their mother's illness, Chris screamed at her, accusing her of trying to get their mother's money by "hiding things." Carol argued, "She is costing me money, she has no money, what would I be trying to get?" Their circular argument began again. "You are always trying to control everything," and "You always have to be the center of attention."

The next day, Chris showed up at the hospital and insisted she was in charge. The hospital staff informed her that Carol had the power of attorney. Chris shrieked in disbelief, promising to get a lawyer, telling the nurses they would be named in the lawsuit. Carol was shaking when she left the hospital, wavering between tears and rage. "It has always been this way," she cried, "Either she gets her way or she makes everyone miserable. I can't take it anymore and I won't continue like this."

Chris only has power when she gets energy from someone's response. Then she can escalate and exaggerate until others are exhausted. If Carol could stop reacting to Chris, the drama between them could wind down.

"So, should I be a saint and pretend nothing bothers me, no matter how hurt I feel? It's not fair," said Carol. No, of course she couldn't do that, but Carol could be herself, her best self; she could use her professional manners.

Carol decided to do what she would like to have done if they were in opposite positions. She decided she would want to be kept abreast of her mother's progress. So she started sending Chris daily e-mail updates. When Chris called, angry as usual, accusing Carol of not telling her everything, Carol's old response would have been to argue, explaining everything that had happened again and again. And, if she left something out in one of the repetitive tellings, Chris would jump on it saying, "There! I knew you were leaving something out; you told me before that . . . " Carol would respond, "I am telling you, and then try to give Chris more details on what was happening."

This time she simply said, "Sorry, that is all I know." Silence. No more words came out of her mouth regardless of what Chris said. Again, Carol relied on good manners and was polite and empathetic, saying things like "Gosh, that's too bad," or "Yes, I know it is hard." In the past, Carol would have defended herself, asking, "Why is it hard for you? You don't even call her," but now she was simply silent as her sister railed on. After a few minutes Chris's fury subsided, and Carol said, "If there is anything else, let me know. I will keep you up-to-date by e-mail. Bye." Chris responded, "Bye."

I know I can only change myself, but I really wanted to change her and make her better.

Carol felt shaky after their conversation, but she didn't feel like crying. She found herself chuckling and proud of herself for treating her sister with respect regardless of how Chris behaved. The transition has begun. Carol feels in control of herself and safe from her sister for the first time in her life. She held herself to her own standard of conduct rather than lowering herself to their usual shrieking match. "It is a new feeling and I like it." "I know," she chuckled, "I can only change myself, but I wanted so much to change her and make her better." Simply making a change in her response to her sister started the transition that will lead to a transformation in their relationship. It will never be what Carol would have wanted, but some relationships should not be intimate or close, some should simply be "nice." Carol pruned—her relationship with her sister.

Pleasure and Passion

Pleasure and passion is the fourth and final stage in transition to transformation. Pleasure is a pleasing feeling or in a more scientific sense it is sensual gratification. A pleasant smell, a soft touch, a lovely sight, a delectable meal, or the lull of a melody. Pleasure is subtle, while passion is a powerful and intense. Passion locks our emotions and our senses into an intense eruption of energy that spreads through the body. Pleasure is optional, passion is obsessive. Fear, anger, disgust, sadness, and joy in their various forms can all be passionate, intense and compelling—beyond reason. Joy is the only emotion that opens the mind and heals the body; it is the key to our creativity.

Pleasure and passion are the opposite of antipathy. Antipathy, or not caring, is unhealthy, and leads to depression or a feeling of being "in limbo," the opposite of **Bounce**. We find pleasure and passion by taking chances. Sometimes we find our passion just doing something new. Nike says, "Just do it"; **Bounce** says, "Just go!"

One thing leads to another and that is how we find our passions. Try it. Do something you have thought about or dreamed of. Or maybe something you saw someone else do. Go ahead, give it a whirl. If nothing else it's a new experience.

An element that adds meaning to pleasure and passion is altruism. Happiness comes from doing what we do well. Intentions don't count; good deeds do. Researchers have found that when people pursue their own pleasure they enjoy the moment, but those who blend their pleasures and passion with helping others have lasting satisfaction. To build on our strengths in what we do and apply those abilities to the benefit of others gives our life both joy and fulfillment—fulfillment that is lasting.

Unfortunately it is impossible to sit back and decide what you can do and where you will find joy and meaning. Take a chance, start with what you know, and see if you like it. If you like it, do it some more; if not, try something else. Transition is part of every change. We don't just start at one place and immediately arrive at another. It is the stretch during transition that creates transformation. We know we have found passion when we forget about ourselves. When we are engaged in our passion, we lose track of the world around us. We forget what time it is. We don't fret or worry or wait for the praise of others. *We find our bliss.*

Pleasure and passion are my reason for writing this book and launching **Bounce**. Logically I cannot account for my desire to write this book. It is certainly not for money. On the contrary, writing the **Bounce** books and starting this program has cost us money.

Ego doesn't fit because I get more ego needs met coaching. And writing or speaking has the risk of being ego-negative: Other people may not like what I write or say. It is passion, and I seem to be compelled to write. When I am seeing clients on the same days I write, I set an alarm. Otherwise I can forget the time.

I find writing more of a passion than a pleasure. It is not joyful in the sense of jumping up and down in glee, but I do enjoy it. Many days I get up eager to write and feel disappointed if there are other things I need to do. Writing is a stretch for me, especially the way these books are done. I create the layout, images and format as I go. Because I include graphics and images I also have to know how to use complex software as well as the Internet.

Every year or two I update my computer, printers and backup system. The whole process is a steep learning curve. And my Achilles heel is organization. I am not a linear thinker and it is hard for me to put things in order. Fortunately I have Judy to organize my books now, but the first year I spent more time organizing and reorganizing than I did writing. Since organization is a struggle for me, having someone else do that allows me to do what I love—writing.

The other passion embedded in writing for me is learning. Fact-checking and making sure that what I believe is supported by evidence beyond my own opinion is important. Learning about the recent advances in understanding the brain, mind, and body through the use of functional magnetic resonance has excited *my* brain and inspired me to learn more. The other challenging and adventurous part of writing is putting thoughts and ideas into practical, useful terms that can be easily understood and implemented by others. And, last but not least, the ideas and how I communicate them have to be simple and elegant enough to be easy and fun, otherwise they are not sustainable.

I didn't just get up one morning and decide to write a book. As I think about my life, I have had many bounces, sometimes because I hit something hard and other times from my own willingness to embrace change. My late teens and early 20s were a tumultuous time. I enrolled in secretarial school at 17 since there was no consideration on my part, or anyone else's for that matter, that I would go to college. The goal in those days was to get married and obtain a "Mrs." degree. I married at age 18. Shortly thereafter my husband was sent to fight in Vietnam.

While he was away, I started nursing school and then worked in a psychiatric hospital as a practical nurse. On the home front, I thought I was being a "good wife" although I didn't really know what that was supposed to mean. My husband soon returned from Vietnam, even more quiet and withdrawn than when he left. I had no real comprehension about what had happened to him, and a year later our marriage ended. I returned to Battle Creek and worked in a mental health unit as a practical nurse, where I met a young psychologist. He was the first highly educated person I had ever known.

We married when I was 22. The term "secondhand" applied to me—a woman who had been married and divorced. I thought that once I had sex with a man, we "had" to get married, and I was grateful that he would marry me. My psychologist husband introduced me to a whole new world of insight, understanding, and change. He led me into one of my biggest life transformations, encouraging me to go to college. I was amazed at how much I liked it!

But the 1970s were a time of social and interpersonal turmoil in America. It was the beginning of the "sexual liberation" movement. Fidelity and monogamy were out. Casual sex and open marriage were in. My Midwest values didn't fit with the changing times, and after seven years of marriage, we divorced.

I married my husband of 30+ years, Lynn, in 1977 at age 29, while in graduate school completing a master's degree in education and starting a Ph.D. My husband's son lived with us. I was excited by the journey of learning, albeit with its personal challenges. A year into our marriage, Lynn's two teenage daughters also came to live with us. It was a time of difficulty, but I enjoyed them and I was glad to have children in my life. All three were struggling and I made the choice to love and support them rather than have my own child. I didn't think I could handle more. Caring for them, creating a new marriage, finishing my Ph.D. and working all in the same time frame was too much, and, as women often do, I put myself last, gained weight, developed insomnia, and was really cranky! I was stressed and got sick easily, often developing pneumonia due to the vulnerability of my lungs. About a year or so later, I realized I couldn't live like that, and the transition began.

I started exercising, stopped overeating, got a dog for my stepson, focused on developing my counseling practice, and reenergized friendships. I took charge of the household and began dealing with the kids directly rather than through Lynn. I developed

I started exercising, stopped overeating, got a dog for my stepson, focused on developing my counseling practice, and reenergized friendships

a friendly relationship with Lynn's ex-wife and we connected as one family. I took over the dinners and homework and we developed some routines. We all regained our equilibrium and as the girls finished high school and left for college, my life got easier. My husband, Lynn, is an internationally renowned pediatric (children's) orthopedist (bone and joint doctor), who is invited to travel throughout the world teaching other doctors the methods of caring for children with bone and joint problems in ways that are least disruptive to young lives. We traveled internationally two to four times a year and made innumerable national trips. Soon long plane rides, social lunches, and shopping became boring. I started to take my computer with me and began to write. I fiddled around trying to write, off and on, for a couple of years, but I couldn't find a focus. Finally, I decided to write booklets on different "facts"—such as *Facts on Marriage, Facts on Divorce*, etc.

A close friend of ours told his wife of 18 years that he had met someone else and wanted a divorce. His wife read countless self-help books, although, at the time, there were *no* books on surviving affairs. She found an assortment of counselors that gave every possible opinion from "kick the jerk out" to "forgive and forget." Everyone had an opinion. So I decided to do some research. All this happened in the 90s before the Internet, so it was libraries and bookstores.

A year or so later, writing part-time, I was stuck until I found someone who knew how to put together a book—Judy Dreis. Judy organized and edited the book. Friends pitched in, reading and commenting. A friend and graphic designer, Angela Turk, created the cover: a little black book with a big red heart in the middle, and we called it *Triangles, Facts on Affairs*. The *Seattle Times* did a story based on the book, and other newspapers nationwide picked up the story. Two more books followed, *Affair-Proof Your Marriage* and *The Complete Idiot's Guide to Affair-Proof Love*. My little book gained popularity and was purchased by HarperCollins in 1997 and retitled *Triangles—Understanding, Preventing and Surviving an Affair*. I enjoyed every aspect of the book tour, television and radio talk shows, and book signings. I hoped that learning more about marital affairs helped people save their marriages—if that was what they wanted. It was one of the most exciting times of my life. It became an unexpected "WOW," with both joy and meaning, and led me into new experiences rich with opportunity to learn and grow.

Life was moving fast and while continuing with my counseling and coaching career, in 2000 to 2003, I was the Founding Board Member of the University of Washington's Center for Women and Democracy whose mission was to support, educate, and empower women throughout the world. As chair of the global networking program, I visited 15 different countries including Latvia, Lithuania, Estonia, Hungary, and Poland.

In response to 9/11, Lynn and I founded Global-HELP—a humanitarian organization dedicated to creating low-cost publications to improve the quality of health care in transitional and developing countries. We believe that much of the suffering and violence throughout the world comes from inequity. One commodity that offers renewable resources is information. Global-HELP provides free health care texts for developing countries worldwide. In 2004, I joined Harvard University's Women's Leadership Board of Directors as well as the International Women's Forum. During the same time, I helped raise $1.5 million for the orthopedic department at Children's Hospital and Medical Center in Seattle, Washington, for which we received a National Philanthropy Award. All of this should have made me exquisitely happy, but I wasn't.

I thought I knew what was best for him.

It was during this busy time that Lynn retired from his career as an orthopedic surgeon and began writing textbooks. He moved his office into our home, where I had *my* office; living and working together in the same space on a daily basis felt oppressive to me. I was frustrated with Lynn for not taking charge of his new life in a way that I thought would make him happy. I did everything I could to get him to see that his life could be better if he would only make a few improvements. I wanted him to change, but of course trying to change him was far more appealing than changing myself. And I was also making the same mistake I have watched women make over and over in relationships—believing I knew what was best for him.

I was able to brainstorm ideas and write small sections of **Bounce**, but I couldn't seem to get the bigger concepts clear in my mind. "Practice what you preach," I reminded myself. Some days, putting one foot in front of the other was all I did, but I knew I had to keep moving. I kept on writing, deleting, editing, rewriting and so on. I changed computers, upgraded my software and created a better workspace for myself. Sometimes, I felt like I was going in circles, but I tried to remind myself to be patient with myself and just focus on the things I enjoyed. I also started pruning relationships—spending less time with people who sapped my energy and more time with people who were interested in new ideas.

Little by little, I discovered a whole new frontier of brain research that supported my experiences helping people change. *Voilà!* Transformational personal change can happen and it need not be complicated or agonizing. In fact, change works better when accompanied by joy. YES! One of the most important lessons from this research and earlier scientific evidence is proof that *what we think determines what we feel, what we do, and how we affect those around us.* It also teaches us that we feel better, learn better, and live better when we are joyful. It was what I was looking for to help me focus my message, but I was still having trouble.

> *Transformational personal change can happen and it need not be complicated or agonizing.*

I sent samples of the manuscript to publishers who declined. I wanted to make what I had learned available to others who may be able to learn a simple way to become their best, so I decided to try and find the people who helped me create *Triangles*—Judy and Angela. And as so often happens when we look, I found them.

It has been about ten years since I have written. My passion for **Bounce** is a pleasure and a joy interspersed with fury and frustration, but at the end of the day it gives my life both joy and meaning.

> *At the end of the day writing gives my life both joy and meaning.*

Pleasure and passion always include a piece of irrationality. It is part of our creative nature to try something new, to do something different, to explore a new feeling or think a new thought. Pursuing pleasure and passion does not mean being irresponsible, but simply pushing the edge of the envelope a little. Without the push there is no joy or meaning, no creativity, no discovery and no change. We stop living and only exist. Seek joy, feel pleasure and find your passions.

FREEDOM

Bounce needs freedom. Freedom is the ability to exercise free will and make choices independent of outside forces. Freedom to bounce means exploring new parts of yourself and your life.

I remember feeling a jolt the first time I heard someone say that rebellion and conformity are two sides of the same coin. "How could they be? Rebellion means freedom to do what I want, while conformity means doing what I am told. I prefer rebellion," I thought. Upon a little more reflection I saw the problem. Neither rebellion nor conformity has freedom. They are both ways of reacting or responding to someone else. Yes, rebellion is defiant, meaning I don't have to do what you say. Conformity means I will do what you say. Freedom is exploring, learning, and thinking for myself with an open mind regardless of what others believe or choose.

I am adding a cautionary story here. Times of transition have some built-in risks. After all, you are not doing things the way you have always done them—the way you know. Using your courage to face fears and accept new challenges is necessary in transformation and it is important to surround yourself with others who will look out for you while you are in transition, but never put yourself in danger.

Rebellion and conformity are two sides of the same coin. Neither has freedom.

Hannah, a 50-year-old woman from our ***Bounce*** Circle told the following story:

Several years ago, I went to a seminar called Freedom from Fear. During the fourth of six sessions, we were asked to write down three of the scariest situations we could imagine. One situation I listed was hitchhiking. Any time I see someone on the roadside thumbing a ride, I shudder. It seems so dangerous. After everyone in my group had revealed their list of fears, the group then chose which fear each person would face. They chose hitchhiking for me because they said I had trouble trusting other people and had a need to be in control. Hitchhiking means trusting others and not being in control. My assignment was to hitchhike at night from Seattle to Everett, 25 miles. I would have no money and no phone.

As I stood at dusk on the roadside, I kept assuring myself I was facing my fears. I waited for what seemed like forever but it was probably only 15 to 20 minutes before a man stopped. I got in the car and asked for a ride to Lynnwood, about halfway to Everett.

I kept telling myself I shouldn't be afraid. The man kept asking me if I needed help, but I was so scared I couldn't talk. I just shook my head "No." The man stopped the car at the first stoplight in Lynnwood and I got out. I whispered a thank you. My heart was pounding so fast, I could barely speak.

I walked about a block then put my thumb up again for a ride. The next car that stopped was driven by a woman, a nurse, who thought I was in trouble. She wanted to take me to my home, but I insisted I complete my assignment and become "master of my fear." She said something I will never forget, "Fear is precious, don't lose it, it may save your life someday." She drove me to Everett, then turned around and drove me home.

When I got home I took a long shower, then sat on my bed and cried. Here I had spent months focusing on getting rid of my fear, thinking it was holding me back, but maybe my fear wasn't the problem.

I started thinking about the times when being afraid had been smart. Yes, there were times when fear had stopped me. I had wanted to go swimming when I was 11 and the other kids all jumped in, but I was afraid. I didn't get in the water. They laughed and made fun of me. Later that summer a kid drowned on that river after getting hung up under some trees that had fallen into the water.

Understanding what my fear means and what good it does me was what I needed to learn. Looking back I was just lucky. Taking the challenge simply to be free from fear could have ended in disaster. I was so foolish. Now I listen to my fear as one voice within me, and it has its place. I also listen to the part of me that loves adventure; that is another voice to be heard. Regardless of what other people want, it is up to me to choose my freedom and use my judgment and intuition to keep myself safe. I found that instead of silencing fears I allow them to guide me, and I consciously make my own choices. This is freedom to me.

"I listen to my fears as one voice within me . . . I allow them to guide me."–Hannah

TETHERS

A tether is a rope or chain that restricts movement. Tethers are both useful and limiting. They keep us grounded and help us stay on track and they also hold us down so we don't float off into the stratosphere. We all have tethers. Our beliefs are tethers. Sometimes we are conscious of them and other times we are unaware of what we believe and how our beliefs affect us. Writing this book I found myself rewriting some pages over and over. I thought about what I was thinking as I reworked the same page. At times, I was thinking, "just do your best." Sounds innocuous, doesn't it? As with many things, doing our best can become a drive for perfection. There is no such thing as perfect. So, I remind myself, good is good enough. Tethers give us both safety and restrictions; they are both good and bad.

We need tethers so that we don't just drift off aimlessly, inadvertently putting ourselves in danger.

Think of a hot air balloon. Once it is filled with air and heat it drifts freely against the sky, moving with earthly forces, wind, and warmth. The balloon would easily drift into dangerous situations, power lines, or trees, or when the winds fail it could come down in the ocean far from land, marooning her passengers.

It is the same with freedom. Freedom simply for the sake of freedom gets us into dangerous situations, like Hannah. In our **Bounce** Circle I asked everyone to list their tethers. The most common tether was "taking care of" . . . other people, places, or things. The who or what they we were taking care of varied from taking care of the house, taking care of the kids, or the garden.

Linda's list started out as short: home and family. As we examined her list it got longer, much longer. We started with home. Cleaning? "Yes," said Linda, "usually on Saturday. Weekdays, I try to pick up around the house, do the dishes, get groceries, put away the groceries, fix dinner, clean the kitchen." Linda thought her list was complete.

Kim questioned, "What about watering the plants, weeding your herb garden, picking up the dry cleaning, ironing, unloading the dishwasher, arranging repairs, shopping for household items, running errands?" Linda answered, "Sure, I do all that too. I don't think of that as taking care of the house, but I guess it is. I am so busy taking care of *everything*, I don't take care of myself."

Kim added, "Laundry wears me out, and not just clothes, towels, sheets and rugs. There is always something that needs to be washed. Especially the windows."

Caring for our homes is one of our most basic needs—safety and security as well as self-esteem—and can also occupy a lot of time and can be an obstacle to growth. My mother-in-law, Letha, used to say, "A clean house is a waste of a woman's mind."

A clean house is a waste of a woman's mind.

Busyness is one of the most powerful tethers against **Bounce.** Nearly everyone talks about how busy they are and it is true. Americans brag about their busyness as though it is valuable. We wear busyness like a badge of honor. It only takes a few minutes of conversation to hear, "I am so busy" . . . with the kids, my parents, the house, the garden, church, friends, work and so on. When our lives are jam-packed with busyness, we cannot possibly have the freedom to bounce.

A friend of mine was an administrative assistant for the CEO of a large manufacturing firm in California. She was relatively new to the job and wanted to prove herself to her boss. She worked extra hours, on her own time, in the evenings and came in early every morning to do extra work.

One morning about 7:00 her boss arrived at the office. He was scheduled to fly out to a meeting in Denver and had accidentally left his plane ticket on his desk.

*Freedom to **Bounce** means removing unnecessary tethers and exploring new parts of yourself and your life under your own guidance, and with an open mind.*

He asked my friend what she was doing at work so early. She told him she was doing extra work to show him what a valuable employee she was. His answer stunned her. "Oh," he said, "I've noticed that you've been coming in early. I just thought you couldn't get your daily work done in the normal work day."

There are many beliefs that we have accepted that may no longer be true, but we haven't updated our thinking. Being wound up in busyness is not admirable or heroic. It means being unhealthy and unhappy. Being wound up means being out of control. We get wound up, stress builds, winding us tighter and tighter; stress is released and we zoom around until all the energy is spent and we run out, stopped cold—just like a wind-up toy.

Change your mind about the romance of being busy and give yourself the freedom to think for yourself. Give your thoughts some thought, then trust your own perceptions. You will know what you need to be healthy and happy, and only you can know what it means to be your best. There are plenty of people in the world telling us what to do, what to think, and what to be. Take the freedom to think for yourself.

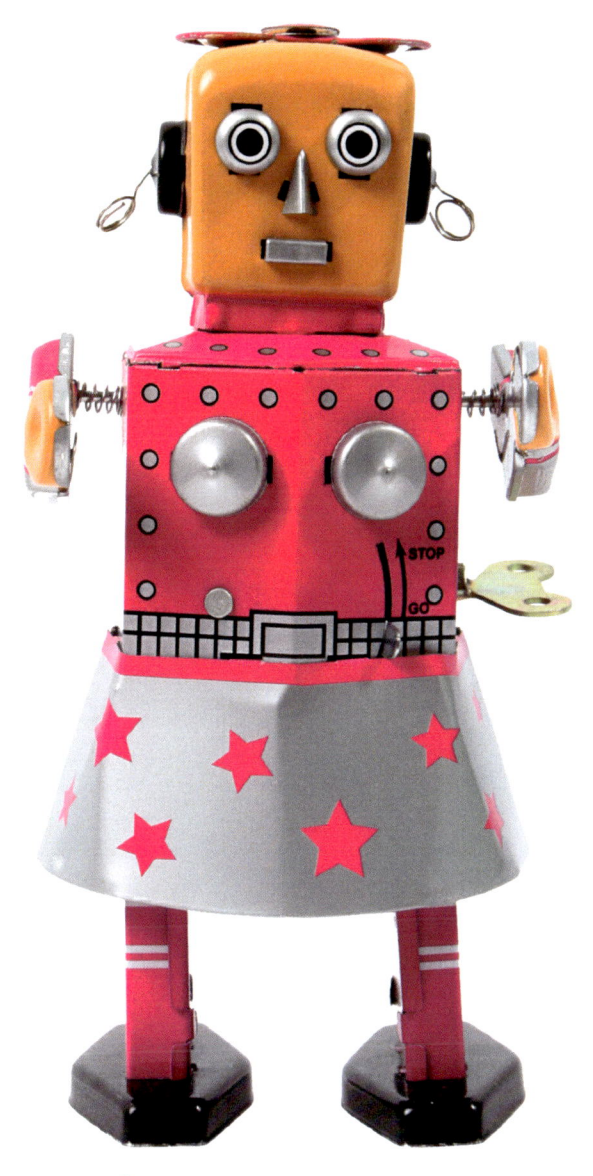

Think about a wind-up toy. It is powered by tightening a small spring using a key. When the spring is released, it unwinds itself trying to get back to its original shape. We wind the key on the toy as far as it will go, then we put it on a hard surface and let go. It quickly speeds straight ahead or around in circles until it runs out of energy and the spring gets back to its original position—then it stops cold, just like us when we are too wound up.

Janice's Bounce

I want to share my story to illustrate how easy and fun it is to bounce, even when you're not faced with a crisis.

I am 50 years old and I have a blessed life, a great husband and wonderful teenagers (as wonderful as teenagers can be). My life is free of financial concerns, I am surrounded by wonderful family and friends, and I am healthy. Before I married for the first time at 38 years old, I had far exceeded my financial and career goals, so my self-esteem was flying high. I had my daughter at age 39 and my son at 41. Who could possibly ask for more? Who wouldn't consider this the kind of life everyone dreams of . . . I surely had.

When I decided to retire and let my business dissolve, some of my friends who had done so before me cautioned me not to completely let it go. "You won't believe how fast your self-esteem will start to dwindle," they warned. I respect my friends. Most of them had their kids at the normal time of life, in their 20s and 30s, so knowing that there must be something to what they were saying, I filed it under "better remember this" and retired anyway.

> *"I realized that it wasn't "more" that I had wanted—I just wanted my energy and natural enthusiasm back!"*

About four years ago, I started noticing that I was low on the energy and enthusiasm that had always been a part of my makeup. A friend called me and invited me to Africa to climb Mt. Kilimanjaro. Once I decided that I would go, I found that my fear of finding myself halfway up the mountain and having to turn back was enough to motivate me to train . . . hard.

I had a goal that involved lots of outdoor exercise and I was feeling great, physically and emotionally, when I went to Africa. When I reached the summit, I was proud of myself. In addition to reaching my goal, I was inspired by the African people.

I told myself that when I got back home everything was going to be different, and it was—for a while. I had a new perspective, a world view, and I had changed. I would be more aware, more giving, more thoughtful of the world, I told myself. About three months later, however, I was using the same old lame reasons to excuse myself from maintaining the fitness level that I had reached. I was using traffic as an excuse to stay holed up all day; and I was growing increasingly annoyed with my husband and snapping at my children. My friends told me I was "going underground."

I was very happy to lie around and read for the better part of my days. I was sure that if we could move to a smaller town, and that if my husband and kids would shape up, everything would be great. But I was unhappy again. Of course I was also burdened with the guilt that comes with being blessed and still wanting more—so I pushed those thoughts out of my mind whenever they surfaced.

I knew I should be "giving back," but all that took was a check to a charity and another to the family I had met in Africa, and I had covered that base (at least that's what I told myself). I had convinced myself that the only people that attended charity events were ones who needed their egos stroked.

I have faced numerous challenges in my life, recognized when I was faced with one, and always used 150% of my resources in solving them successfully. At 50, I knew how to manage life's trials—or so I thought.

One day I got an invitation from Dr. Lana Staheli, whose counseling had been instrumental in helping me make good life and career decisions years earlier. Our relationship had morphed from doctor/patient to friendship, but I hadn't spent time with her for a long time. She invited me to her 60th birthday bash. I almost declined at the prospect of the wasted hours I would have to spend in traffic, but out of gratitude and friendship I decided that I had to attend.

Lana later confessed that her motive for pulling me out of my life was that she needed me to help her work on finishing and launching her new book. Feeling incredibly indebted for the years she had helped me, of course, I couldn't say "No."

*"What is this **Bounce** thing?" I wondered before I went to see her. The website looked like it had something to do with Children's Hospital and the emotional trauma associated with illness. Oh no! She wants me to get involved in a charity thing with a group of women. How could she? She knows me better than that. But that wasn't what she wanted. She said, "I need about four days of your time." I only had about an hour, but we started talking.*

*The second time we got together I was finally able to spend enough time with her to gain an understanding of what **Bounce** was all about.*

We talked, went to lunch by boat, and brainstormed on the deck of her tiny houseboat on Lake Union. Lana shared the latest research articles about the advancements they are making in understanding how the brain works.

These articles clearly illustrated that you really can change the wiring in your mind and change your life. Within about four hours that day I found myself fascinated and revved up. Hmmm. That night I drove home thinking that the only way I could support Lana in this venture was if I really believed in it. I had asked her the question, "What's new about these concepts? Isn't this just another "self-help" book with a scientific backdrop?" Good question. We were both going to think about how to answer it.

It has only been about two weeks since I started working on this project and my life has completely transformed. I never would have thought it could be this easy. Lana is right, it is also fun! I have my energy back, I treat my family differently, and the funny thing is that they treat me differently too. My husband responds to me as though he got his girlfriend back; and I am driving, in traffic, to see my friends. I came into this knowing most of the concepts, yet

I just hadn't experienced what it would be like if you put them all together in the way that Lana was suggesting. I could see why Lana wanted to share this. I realized that it wasn't "more" that I had wanted; I just wanted my energy and natural enthusiasm back. And it's back! I am thrilled that I can now "give back," in my own way.

The answer to the question, "Is this just another self-help book?" is "No." As a matter of fact, if the entire world approached life in this way, we surely wouldn't be destroying the planet or killing each other. I invite others to give it a whirl. At the very least, it's fun. —Janice

Janice got her bounce back! Janice's experiment to test **Bounce** was to get everyone she encountered in the course of the day to smile—that's right, smile. I love this part of her story. She actually stood grinning in front of the scowling grocery checker until the woman asked her if there was a problem. Janice explained her mission. The woman laughed so hard she had tears running down her cheeks. "You really care if I smile? Wow! O.K. I'll smile," she said. They both laughed, as did everyone else in line. Everyone that Janice met that day, including her family, was greeted with her smile and she stood there grinning quite a while if necessary until they smiled back. Janice said it was the most fun she had ever had in an ordinary day!

I believe that a main reason for the rapid success of **Bounce** is that it is so easy. Judy, my editor and newest member of **Bounce**, found that learning and implementing **Bounce** was not only easy but also immediate. She writes, *Serendipity, karma or extremely good fortune brought Lana Staheli back into my life after 14 years. She had tracked me down and wanted me to work with her again, organizing and editing her newest book,* Bounce, Be Transformed.

My life had been one of fear and anxiety for four years since I found myself unemployed for the first time, at age 58. I hadn't realized that it was the structure of a job that kept me functioning in the real world. Appearance can be deceiving. My public self was confident, assured, and in control; inside I was depressed, anxious, and full of self-doubt.

Lana had sent me a draft of her book to look over, and I drove up to Seattle to talk with her about it. That first day we talked about the importance of my thinking intentionally about the things I could do to put joy and fulfillment back in my life. "Don't think about the stresses, think about the joy" she said. "Whatever you think about is what will happen." She also gave me a 30-minute meditation tape to listen to that night before I went to bed.

*My transformation began that first day—rather night. I slept for 7 hours, something I hadn't done in years, and woke rested, not anxious—and with a sense of peace and joy I thought I had lost and would never find again. Now I'm **Bouncing** along toward a very different life. I have laughed a lot; I am losing weight; I am more rested and relaxed; and there is joy in my life.*

*Thank you, Lana, and all the other inspiring **Bounce** women; and thank you **Bounce**!*

Life Is a Ball

When a ball is fully inflated, it is well-rounded and it bounces. It has energy, it is a little unpredictable and it is lively and fun.

If a ball is underinflated, it falls flat and lifeless, and it doesn't bounce. It is still a ball, but it isn't much fun.

An overinflated ball is hard, it bounces really well, but it is highly unpredictable and other people don't like to play with it because it hurts when the ball hits them. The ball is always under stress, and one day it comes apart at the seams and it isn't a ball anymore.

Like a ball, our lives can be underfilled, overfilled, or well-rounded.

When life is underinflated and not all of our needs are met, we are flat and lack energy. We look and feel flat, and life just isn't fun.

When life is overfilled, it may look OK, but it is hard. We are stressed, and other people don't like to be around because they get hurt. Eventually, we come apart at the seams and it isn't much of a life anymore.

When life is well-rounded, our needs are met, friends like to be around, and we have fun. Joy and purpose are parts of everyday life and we have bounce!

Life is a ball!

Core Emotions

Bounce is based on the idea that by managing our thinking, we can change what we feel, what we do, and positively affect the world around us. Nature has given us all we need to change our thinking and transcend what is and move forward toward being our best. Opening our minds to new ideas and ways of thinking keeps us learning and growing, leading to personal transformations, allowing us to explore the complexity of the world around and within us.

Our core emotions are fear, anger, disgust, sadness and joy. Our senses act like radar, constantly scanning the world around us to alert us to any sign of danger, then transmitting that information directly to the most primitive part of the brain. This process triggers core emotions.

We are all born with the same core emotions and core needs, designed to insure our survival. Beyond survival we have growth needs and our emotions are there to guide us.

The problem with this primitive brain wiring is that in today's world we are not fighting a day-to-day battle to stay alive. But life can change instantly. You can be driving the freeway enjoying your favorite music when suddenly a car cuts in front of you. You are startled. It is only an inconvenience, not life-threatening, unless your response escalates into full-blown anger, even rage. Then you may, in fact, be in a life-threatening situation, not because of the other driver but because core survival emotions like anger trump everything. It isn't rational, but when the brain gets a signal that there is a threat, the message goes directly to fight, flight, freeze or surrender, and doesn't even come close to the thinking parts of the brain. During this survival reaction, the brain calls for steroids.

Steroids and endorphins are hormones that signal your body to respond to your thinking. Steroids are potent drugs, increasing strength, stamina, and endurance. Your body produces steroids when you frown, get mad, or grit your teeth. High levels of steroids day-to-day are linked to heart disease, cancer, stroke, accidental death, diabetes, obesity, etc. Endorphins strengthen the immune system, repair cells, relieve pain, counter the affects of aging. They are better than the fountain of youth.

Endorphins are created by what we do, like exercise. What we think—positive thoughts, and what we feel—joy. Endorphins are nature's miracle drug for repairing both brain and body. When we don't use our higher levels of thinking, we will revert to our most primitive core emotions and it is easy to get stuck there, letting one incident ruin your day. And the more you think about and talk about your upset, the deeper and more persistent the memory becomes, leading to a heavy dose of steroids.

Endorphins are better than the fountain of youth.

Endorphins add to our sense of happiness.

CORE EMOTIONS FOR SURVIVAL

Emotions are nature's early warning signal. Nature has given us everything we need not only to survive but also to rebound from hardship. We sense danger and know when to hide, we defend ourselves from animals many times larger than ourselves, we attack enemies, and we recoil from the stench of foul food. We grieve our losses and disappointments and we laugh with abandon. We keep ourselves safe from harm and we repair our bodies and heal our minds. Nature gave us *core emotions,* those that every human possesses. Core emotions give us the foundation for everything we need.

Our senses—sight, sound, smell, taste, and touch—scan the world around us and send the brain raw input. Billions of signals go from the senses down one chemical pathway or another within the brain. Emotions filter these signals and highlight the ones that are important to our survival. When the senses transmit chemical signals that remind the brain of danger, we feel fear.

The brain doesn't mess around with fear. The senses directly signal the most primitive part of the brain, the amygdala. The brain then sends messenger cells, called steroid hormones, to the body. When the body gets a big shot of steroids, we are ready for fight, flight, freeze or surrender. Emotions insure our survival. They are immediate, and don't involve any thought. All of this happens without our conscious awareness, accounting for the quickness of our emotions and the discrepancies between our thinking and our feelings.

It is our emotions that tell us where to focus, and survival is always our first priority. For that reason, four of our five hard-wired emotions, fear, anger, disgust and sadness, trigger the release of steroids. Steroid hormones give us energy boosts, strength, and exceptional abilities. They give us our get-up-and-go. Harking back to "cave" days, humans needed fear to know when to run if surprised by a woolly mammoth. Anger was necessary to motivate us to fight to protect our food or our families; disgust caused us to recoil from harmful tastes or smells; and sadness slowed the brain so it could cleanse and restore itself. Excessive levels of steroid hormones, however, are linked to ailments that lessen our quality of life and lead to disease and early death.

10 Leading Causes of Death
Heart disease
Malignant neoplasms—cancer
Cerebrovascular diseases—stroke
Chronic lower respiratory diseases
Unintentional injuries—accidents
Dibetes mellitus
Influenza and pneumonia
Alzheimer's disease
Nephritis, nephrotic disease—kidneys
Septicemia—blood infection

Joy is the only core emotion that triggers endorphins. Endorphins are also messenger hormones. These messenger cells repair damaged cells, restore full brain activity and slow aging. Our thinking is the most original and creative during or soon after feeling joy. Seek joy to be happy and creative.

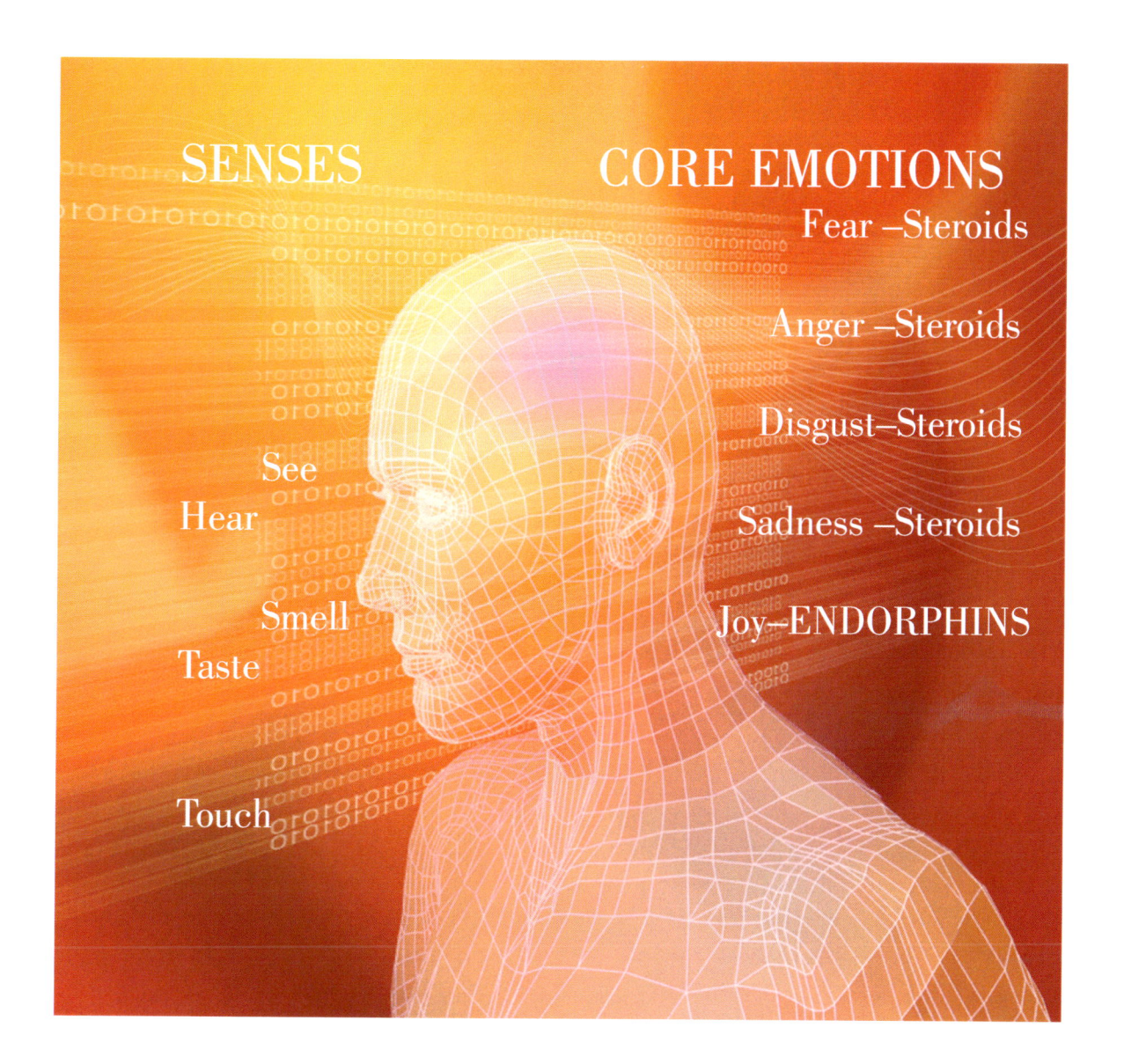

SENSES	CORE EMOTIONS
	Fear –Steroids
	Anger –Steroids
	Disgust–Steroids
See	
Hear	Sadness –Steroids
Smell	Joy–ENDORPHINS
Taste	
Touch	

Our five senses—sight, sound, smell, taste, and touch—signal the brain. Five core emotions—fear, anger, disgust, sadness and joy—point us in the direction we should focus our attention. The brain responds by sending stress hormones, steroids, or endorphins, telling the body what to do: either rev up, or rest and repair.

LEARNED EMOTIONS

In our "cave" days, staying alive was a day-to-day challenge, and being vigilant about possible danger was more important than feeling good. Hence four of our five hard-wired emotions rev us up, and only one heals, soothes and repairs. It makes sense that if Mr. Caveman sees a woolly mammoth nearing his camp, it would be better to respond with fear and run, even if he is wrong. Seeing the woolly mammoth and thinking "Oh, someone new to play with, yippee!" could be right, but being wrong could be fatal.

Over time we have developed and refined our emotions to adapt to different dangers and to have emotions that require less energy. In other words our brains conserve energy and operate efficiently. Emotions are grouped into three major categories: *core emotions, learned emotions,* and *background emotions*. Core emotions—fear, anger, disgust, sadness and joy—are present in every human, and unshaped by culture or society.

Learned emotions give us social, cultural, and interpersonal cues for coping with the complexity of daily life—cues that last a lifetime.

Learned emotions are emotional responses that develop over a lifetime and are refinements of core emotions. The initial emotion trigger comes from the senses. If you eat something you have not tasted before and enjoy it, your brain creates a memory of your senses: the taste, the smell, the look, or the sound. Later when your senses identify the same smell, look or taste, you instinctively know you will probably like it. The information from the first experience is embedded in your brain and you don't have to think consciously whether you will like it or not. This sensing process—gut feeling or intuition—is learned without our awareness.

Learned emotion is shaped by modern experience, but is also an adaptation for immediate survival. These emotions tell the brain in a general way whether the message is good or bad. For instance, "Is the approaching person friend or foe?" "Should I smile and greet him or ignore him?" This sense of good or bad gives us choices. Men are faster to respond to risk than women, but women are more accurate in assessing actual risk than men.

Learned emotions give us social, cultural and interpersonal cues for coping with the complexity of daily life. Learned emotions leave markers in the front part of the brain so that when the brain receives a similar cue later, the response is faster and requires less energy each time. We often think of this as intuition. The body reacts to the similarity of the new to the previous messages and the outcome tied to that message. So, if a peculiar sound reminds a woman of the time she was hit by her former boyfriend, she will shrink away in fright when she hears that same sound regardless of the current situation.

Sometimes we meet someone we feel we have known forever; we might call them a soul mate. You don't need to think about why you like them because you feel connected. These feelings are triggered by the brain's response to markers from previous emotions. You're probably not aware of the markers. It may be the person's scent (pheromones); a look in their eyes; or familiarity of their energy. We respond to these signals because of our markers.

The third type of emotion is *background emotion*. The brain and body are in a resting state. Background feeling is like emotional radar; it scans the mind, body, and environment, and only responds to change.

Background feeling is your emotional neutral. Most of our day-to-day life is spent on background mode. We are on cruise control, but with the senses always scanning the physical and emotional landscape. Core and learned emotions take energy, and the mind and body are programed to conserve energy, spending their resources only as necessary.

The scope and scale of everyday life gives us a level of stimulation from numerous contact with dozens of other people throughout the day, and millions of bits of information coming at us by Internet or television. At no time in human history has the human brain processed more information daily. Danger from a hungry tiger has been replaced by reckless drivers or gun-wielding gangs. But most of our day-to-day dangers are merely annoyances or disappointments that do not really require huge doses of steroids to insure our basic survival.

We can use our thinking to manage our learned emotions and distinguish when we are in fact in real danger and when we are simply being inconvenienced or disappointed. Perhaps one of the best ways to find joy is through play. Playing is to amuse oneself with no real purpose other than one's own pleasure. It is an opportunity to be creative and it often leads to one of my favorite experiences—laughter.

> *We have the ability to change our emotions and, through experience, continue to evolve and think new thoughts.*

It is the interaction of core, learned, and background emotion that allows us to create and cope with many of the complexities of life. Rather than simply instinctual survival emotions, we have layers of emotion and thought intertwined.

It is our ability to draw from our emotions that allows us to navigate through new situations. We have the ability to *change* our emotions and, through experience, continue to evolve and think new thoughts. Needs which are met are "silent"; they don't speak to us. Our emotions help us identify and manage our feelings so we can address those needs which are unmet and which are preventing us from moving forward to a life of joy and fulfillment.

Core Needs

Every human being has the same hard-wired needs, just as we all have the same hard-wired emotions. Looking back at our "cave" days gives us perspective on why we are the way we are. Our so-called hard wiring, those pathways inside the brain that are present in every human being, have developed over thousands of years of genetic modification. In the late 1940s, psychologist Abraham Maslow theorized that all humans have the same biological and psychological needs—basic requirements that all of us must have met to survive and thrive. Our core emotions insure our core needs.

Psychological needs include safety needs, e.g., security, stability, structure, law and order. Our interpersonal needs include the need to belong, or to be associated with other people. We need to love and be loved, to have a sense of caring and affection for others.

Self-esteem needs include feelings of respect, achievement, and appreciation. Cognitive needs involve the desire to know, learn, explore, and create. We have the need to increase knowledge and our understanding.

All humans have the same biological and psychological needs—basic requirements that all of us must have met to survive and thrive.

Our aesthetic needs involve appreciation of art and beauty, and a desire to experience pleasure through our senses—hearing, seeing, touching, smelling, or tasting. We have the ability to experience all emotions through art.

The ongoing grass roots drive for personal growth supports Dr. Maslow's theory that growth needs are as important as any other need. We are continually driven to understand ourselves and those around us, and to be better.

Growth needs include personal and spiritual growth and self-transcendence. Self-actualization, a growth need, means going beyond the self for the well-being of others, and often does not develop until the person is 50 or older. We are at our best when we are in continuous transformation.

Each set of needs is layered. Once we go through the complete cycle of needs, we go through the same set again at a new level. So, once we have a nice cave, plenty to eat, a consistent set of social rules, a feeling of connection with family, a sense of our own skills and abilities, and an attitude of unselfishness we can move to a bigger cave, befriend neighbors not just family, love a larger circle of people, gain greater more diverse levels of competence, and be more open, playful, and generous with other people and societies.

Self-transcendence is the ability to go beyond self-gratification, giving an individual a sense of purpose beyond their own life. Spiritual needs, an acceptance of an individual's place in the universe, fit in this category.

Growth needs are perpetual—they are never completely met—but as we pass through each level we find satisfaction, gratitude, and inner peace unlike anything we have known before. The journey of growth is **Bounce**, it is being our best self. The drive to bounce is deeply rooted in who we are. Our desire for personal growth is universal and timeless. It contains the seeds of our dissatisfaction with the way things are. It gives us the desire for a better life, a better society, and a better self.

Needs can easily change into wants, and wants interfere with movement to the next level of need fulfillment. It is impossible to become self-transcendent while shopping for another new outfit. Before you gasp in disbelief that I am suggesting no more shopping, I am not—only that you choose thoughtfully to satisfy your wants, and that you invest in meeting your needs. Meeting needs is gratifying, and not destructive.

We are driven to meet all of our needs, starting with our most basic and primitive survival needs. Once our physical needs are met, we can move up the ladder to social needs then ego needs. It is our need for personal growth, self-actualization and transcendence that gives us ***bounce***.

Maslow's List of Needs

Biological needs
Safety needs
Belonging needs
Need to love and be loved
Self-esteem needs

Cognitive and Aesthetic needs exist at every level

Cognitive needs
Aesthetic needs
Self-transcendence

BIOLOGICAL NEEDS

- *Breathe*
- *Sleep*
- *Regulate body temperature*
- *Regulate body functions*
- *Dispose of waste*
- *Food*
- *Water*
- *Sex*

Needs are requirements. Yes, breathing, sleeping, drinking water are obvious needs. Of course you do these activities without thinking, right? Or do you do just enough to survive? Do you meet your most basic needs appropriately?

Do you breathe deeply, using your entire lung capacity?

Do you pay attention to your body temperature and to your digestive processes?

Do you eat five or six small meals each day?

And, perhaps most important, do you get eight to nine hours of sleep each night? Sleep deprivation is one of the most effective means of torture, confusing the brain and preventing neurons from repairing themselves. Sleep deprivation, meaning "getting by" with five, six or seven hours of sleep is self-imposed torture. Not a good choice!

Are you enjoying sex weekly? Do you usually have orgasms?

These needs are priorities and should be met at the highest level, not just good enough. Biological needs are requirements, meaning they must be met for us to be able to move to the next level of our well-being. They cannot be denied or postponed without interfering with the workings of both mind and body. Think about how well you meet your needs in each of these categories.

SAFETY AND SECURITY NEEDS

- *Physical security*
- *Safety from violence*
- *Security of work*
- *Security of resources*
- *Moral and physiological security*
- *Family safety*
- *Security of health*
- *Security of property against crime*

Safety and security ranks second in the hierarchy of needs. Survival is more important than friendship or love.

The belief that we are safe is the opposite of feeling fear, giving us the opportunity to move forward to meet other needs. Safety gives us a sense of predictability. When we are safe we believe our home will still be our home tomorrow; we do not worry that someone is going to suddenly arrive with guns and throw us out.

Safety and security needs are met through social mores and laws that governments endorse and enforce. Social mores dictate specific codes of conduct. American women can expect to drive to work without being arrested for driving, as is the case in some countries, because as a society we have chosen for women to have this freedom.

It is laws and rules that are enforced with uniformity that give us the greatest sense of safety and security, allowing us to focus our energy on other needs.

Belonging Needs

- *Kinship, family, friends*
- *Joining clubs, gangs*
- *Sense of community*
- *Commitment to group*
- *Church membership*

    Feeling connected to others is the number two criteria for happiness. People need a few other people with whom they have emotional connections. We think and talk of "loners" as people who are sad, forlorn, even dangerous. The rapist and murderer Ted Bundy; Theodore Kaczynski, the man known as the Unabomber; and Adolph Hitler—were all loners.
    Human beings are tribal, and our ability to work together and share resources has enhanced our survival. When we join groups, we agree to the rules or beliefs prescribed by that group and surrender some of our independence in exchange for belonging. Finding the balance between belonging and independence is the key to happiness and need fulfillment.

Need to Love and Be Loved

- *Affectionate relationships with family and friends*
- *Individual intimacy*
- *Committed friendships*
- *Care and nurturing of young and old*

Loving and feeling loved is a drive laced with romance, mystery and sexual intimacy. There is, of course, the in-love feeling that lasts anywhere from a few weeks to a few years that is intense, but temporary. For those with lasting marriages this period is followed by sexual and emotional intimacy that can last a lifetime if nurtured.

There is filial love between parent and child that is as unconditional a love as human beings obtain. Other types of love include a sense of brotherhood or sisterhood; caring for and nurturing young and old.

Need for Self-Esteem

- *Recognition from self and others*
- *Respect*
- *Confidence*
- *Competence*
- *Appreciation*
- *Achievement*

We are social beings and what other people think about us and say to us makes a difference in how we view ourselves—our self-esteem. Knowing that others hold us in high regard inspires us to be better. Ultimately it is what we think and believe about ourselves that determines our self-image and esteem.

Our drives to know and understand, learn and explore build self-esteem. Self-esteem does not grow without new learning and new experiences. We gain esteem by testing and retesting ourselves.

Self-Transcendence

As we pass through each level of needs, the next level comes into focus. From safety we move to belonging, from belonging to love, from love to self-esteem, from self-esteem to self-transcendence, and from self-transcendence to self-actualization. We have an internal drive to be our best.

Transcendence, meaning going beyond the present self, requires balance and closure. We strive for internal harmony—meeting needs with a minimum amount of energy in order to have the resources to pass beyond what is and continue our personal growth.

Self-transcendence means going past your own ego and needs to embrace change that benefits others. It is within each of us to better ourselves. We chose eight women as examples of self-transcendence. Each of these women passed up opportunities for material wealth or personal power to do something for the benefit of humankind. Each woman struggled and pursued a dream beyond herself.

1. Mother Teresa—founder of the ***Missionaries of Charity*** in Calcutta, India. ***Mother Teresa's Missionaries of Charity*** continued to expand to 610 missions in 123 countries.
2. Eleanor Roosevelt—advocate for civil rights; enhanced the status of working women; a co-founder of **Freedom House** and supporter of the formation of the **United Nations**.
3. Jane Goodall—established the ***Jane Goodall Institute*** which supports research in the effort to protect chimpanzees and their habitats.
4. Melinda French Gates—co-founder and co-chair of the ***Bill & Melinda Gates Foundation*** embodies the belief that every life has equal value. They have contributed over $16 billion toward helping people live healthy productive lives.
5. Oprah Winfrey—TV mogul and the most philanthropic African American of all time, creating an educational foundation, relief for victims of Katrina, and a leadership academy for girls in South Africa.
6. Maya Angelou—poet laureate and author of ***I Know Why the Caged Bird Sings*** and one of the first African American women to write about her personal life. She is recognized as an advocate for blacks and women.
7. Sandra Day O'Connor—the first woman to serve on the Supreme Court, who set aside her own political views to consider cases on individual merit. She is an outspoken critic of a politicized Supreme Court.
8. Nancy Brinker—founder of the ***Susan G. Komen Race for the Cure®***, created a relationship between the business community, government, and volunteer sectors to fund research for the cure of breast cancer. They have awarded 1,100 breast cancer research grants totaling more than $400 million.

- *Spiritual awareness*
- *Personal growth*
- *Integration*
- *Universal values*
- *Transcendence of self*

Self-transcendence leads to self-actualization in Maslow's theory. Self-actualization is a state of being that includes a clear sense of self—being spontaneous, present in the moment, creative and full of humor. Self-actualized people meet their basic needs efficiently and live simplified lives focusing on problems that disrupt the lives of others. They seek practical solutions without prejudice. Their focus goes beyond themselves and is not motivated by their self-interest. They change themselves and they change the world.

Cognitive Needs

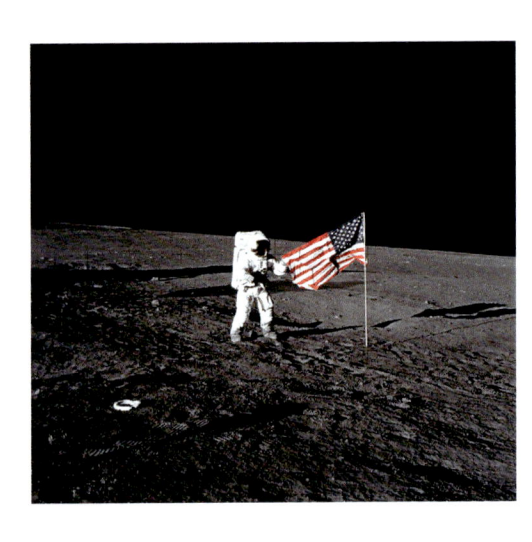

- *Knowledge*
- *Intelligence*
- *Understanding*
- *Wisdom*
- *Appreciation*
- *Achievement*

Cognitive needs refers to our desire for knowledge or facts, and beyond simply knowing a fact is understanding the application of the information. While it may be nice to know something, it is best to understand how to use what you know.

It is our cognitive needs that drive us to think new thoughts and embrace new ideas. It is in our nature to continue searching for new ways—perhaps in the form of understanding the situations of other people, or in having an idea to solve a problem plaguing others. It is what pushes us to extend ourselves beyond what we can know, and explore the universe.

AESTHETIC NEEDS

- *Appreciation of beauty*
- *Symmetry and order*
- *Artistic sensitivity to form*
- *Balance*
- *Closure*

"Musicians must make music, artists must paint, and writers must write," said Dr. Maslow. Aesthetic needs demand that we use our abilities to their fullest. Maslow believed that once the lower level needs were met, our aesthetic needs would drive us, giving us a sense of restlessness or a preoccupation in thinking. "When we are driven by aesthetic needs we cannot get our thoughts off that which we are capable of doing or creating," he wrote.

All humans have the same needs and the same emotions—modified and renamed by cultures, society, families, and individuals, but all emotions come from these basic five: fear, anger, disgust, sadness and joy. All needs involve basic biology, safety, and security, the need to belong and to love and be loved, self-esteem, and transcendence to self-actualization. Core emotions are designed to insure that our core needs are met. We do not survive or thrive unless each set of needs is met, one after another.

Our core needs do not vary from culture to culture, but core emotions do. Emotions valued in one culture sometimes meet with severe disapproval in another. In Japan, public expression of anger is frowned upon while in the U.S. expressing anger is seen as a strength.

I'm going to explain the impact of our most powerful core emotions, fear and anger, together because in today's world they are so intertwined that they are hard to separate. For instance, we rarely hear anyone say, "I feel afraid when you criticize me." Instead we get angry, usually defending ourselves with a counterattack, transferring fear to anger. Many of us would prefer being mad to being afraid. The problem is when we express the wrong feeling we elicit an emotion we don't want from others. Let me give you an example.

Gina and Gary are driving to work, and Gina thinks Gary is driving too fast, so she says in an irritated tone, "Slow down, you are going too fast!" Gary flashes back, "You want to be on time don't you?" Gina answers, "Yes, and I want to get there alive!" Gary's reply? "If you had been ready to go on time we wouldn't have to worry about being late!" Both Gina and Gary are angry and he doesn't slow down. In fact he drives a bit faster.

If Gina had said, "I am afraid, Gary!" she would have been expressing a core need—something that Gary would be more likely to empathize with and respond to favorably. Most men would slow down and comfort someone else, but even if Gary didn't slow down, at least he would not be distracted by accelerating emotions that block clear thinking.

All core emotions interfere with thinking. The very same emotions designed to help us survive are the ones that can cause us harm. Fear is the most powerful human emotion—our first line of defense for any threat. The fear mechanism is the first alert of danger, bypassing all thinking, triggering immediate fight or flight. The brain's fear trigger can get stuck in the "on" position and lead to relentless fear, causing anxiety and depression. Because fear is the most powerful and primitive of our core emotions, it short-circuits the best and brightest minds. Think about the impact of a therapist in the U.S. encouraging patients to express anger in the belief that "getting your anger out" would make people feel better. Scientists have now proven that expressing anger not only doesn't relieve it, expressing anger or any other feeling generates more of that feeling. In other words, shouting out your anger only makes you more angry and makes other people uncomfortable.

During my lifetime, the United States has started two wars because we were afraid. In Vietnam we were "afraid" that if one country in Asia fell to Communism, all would fall—the so-called "domino theory." More recently, the invasion of Iraq was based on the premise that we "feared" Sadam Hussein's "weapons of mass destruction." Fear is more motivating than any other emotion, and often causes us to behave in ways that are not in our own best interest.

Disgust is disapproval through our senses, like a revolting smell or nauseating taste. The smell of vomit or decaying flesh makes us instinctively draw away, even squelching an involuntary gag. It is also a psychological judgment when we criticize behavior or beliefs. For instance, "How could she kiss that jerk and let him grope her in public? That's disgusting!"

Sadness is a natural emotion that allows us to experience and learn from mistakes, loss, or disappointment and then resume our normal activity. Some regions of the brain actually become less active, leaving the person feeling foggy. Sadness, like all core emotions, should be brief and transient.

Joy restores mind and body. Joy is found in many emotions—love, humor, hope, faith, gratitude, forgiveness, silliness, and laughter. All create endorphins, healing the mind and body. Joy is simple, and like all other emotions fleeting. Everyday joy is essential for health, well-being, clear thinking, and a peaceful world.

It is the interaction of core, social, and background emotions that allows us to create and cope with many of the complexities of life. Rather than simply instinctual survival emotions, we have layers of emotion and thought intertwined. We can feel exhilaration and devastation or bliss and distress. We can love and we can worry. We experience a smorgasbord of emotion all within seconds of each other, all based on what we think, whether we are conscious of it or not. It takes a small effort and intent to choose what you feel and how you meet your needs.

Core needs will prevail. They will surface and resurface until they are met. It is easy to confuse wants with needs, but one indicator is addiction. Does getting more leave you wanting more? More clothes, more cars, more money? Core emotions can hijack energy and interfere with meeting needs accurately and efficiently. Meeting needs with the minimum amount of energy paves the way for transformation.

Check to be sure your core needs are being met on a daily, weekly and annual basis.

Endorphins—Nature's Miracle Drugs

Nature has provided us with an antidote to fear, anger, disgust, and sadness: It is joy. We are natural pleasure-seekers. We look for ways to feel good. Pleasurable activities, such as exercising, sex, laughter, touch, and eating chocolate create endorphins. Endorphins are stress-relieving hormones that act much like the opiate drugs opium, morphine, and heroin.

Endorphins produce four key effects on the body and mind: They enhance the immune system, relieve pain, reduce stress, and postpone aging.

Endorphins give the mind and body a dose of painkillers unequaled by modern medications. Many describe this endorphin release as a "rush." Others refer to this feeling as a nervous stomach or queasy feeling. Endorphins give us a visceral response—the mind and body shifting gears, from the familiar to the unfamiliar.

Endorphins, nature's miracle drugs, help mind and body by enhancing the immune system, relieving pain, disrupting the stress cycle, and slowing the aging process.

Endorphins are produced through a wide range of activities—from exercise to meditation, deep breathing, belly laughter, eating spicy food, acupuncture treatments and chiropractic adjustments. Sugar, caffeine, and chocolate contain anandamide, a chemical that mimics marijuana's soothing effects on the brain

Chocolate is by far the most fun and most popular way of producing endorphins. Chocolate was called "food of the gods" by the Greeks and the Aztecs who believed it was a source of wisdom and vitality. Today, chocolate lovers call the effect of endorphins their "inner glow."

The mind and body depend on endorphins to counter the effects of steroids. Steroids place emphasis or stress on our mind and body, and that emphasis or intensity causes damage at a cellular level. It is the balance between steroids and endorphins that gives us our get-up-and-go and our ability to stop and feel joyful in the moment. Endorphins give us a natural high.

We need endorphins as part of our daily life as well as during trying times. When we keep up our endorphin levels we are ready for whatever comes our way. We are always ready to **Bounce!**

Endorphins—the Natural High

It may seem strange, but . . .

in times of stress we suggest that you

smile and laugh,

hug and kiss,

sing and dance,

have a massage,

get your hair done,

and . . .

EAT CHOCOLATE!

Aztecs, Incas, French and Latins all share one special food—cocoa. Cocoa powder is produced by roasting and grinding cacao beans.

The cocoa powder generally served in the United States is about 7% cocoa butter, but special cocoa powders contain approximately 12%-24% and ice cream/dessert manufacturers can use cocoa powder with up to 33% cocoa butter, adding lots of calories and perhaps eliminating the benefit.

Eat chocolates, they are simple and bite-sized.

It is rarely true that something this good is actually good for you, but chocolate containing 70% cocoa is—in moderation of course. Add a little milk and have a hot or cold treat.

BETTER THAN NARCOTICS FOR PAIN

Endorphins are better than narcotics for pain. People who are able to create endorphins naturally experience less pain and heal faster than those who worry about their pain. Worry creates steroids that worsen the experience of pain, while *endorphins relieve pain and promote healing.*

What we think also changes the pain we feel, physically. A research study at the University of Michigan Medical School with patients who were experiencing pain showed that the body could actually produce its own narcotic-like hormones—endorphins.

The so-called placebo effect is one where a person's symptoms are relieved because they believe that a meaningless treatment is making them better. In this study the patients were told that new highly effective pain medication had been injected into the body when actually nothing was administered. They were "high" on endorphins. The results of the UM study provided the first direct evidence that endorphins—the brain's own pain-relieving chemicals—play a role in the placebo effect.

Better Than the Fountain of Youth

Endorphins postpone aging, leaving us looking and feeling younger. Research has also shown that some of the activities that we do to make ourselves look better actually create endorphins. Touching and being touched creates endorphins, so if you enjoy having your hair styled, your nails manicured, your feet pedicured, or a hand or foot massage, just go! You create endorphins from touch as well as from the pleasure you get from the thought that you are taking good care of yourself.

Greeks and Romans sucked on anise seed to peak their sexual appetite. The smell of almonds is reported to create arousal in women, while bananas assist the development of sex hormones for both men and women. Some believe celery contains hormones that are arousal stimulants for men. Basil is considered by some to be a feel-good herb, and the oldest aphrodisiac is thought to be cilantro. While not as powerful, mustard, asparagus, carrots, licorice, and vanilla are believed to inspire desire. Now you know! It's food for thought. There really is such a thing as brain food; they are antioxidants. The brain is about 60% fat, making it the human organ with the highest percentage of fat. Human fat holds many toxins generated from what we eat, the air we breathe, our daily stresses, and normal aging. Antioxidants help cleanse fat of toxins. The single best source of antioxidants? Blueberries!

The Harvard Nurses' Health Study reports that women who ate the most broccoli, cauliflower, kale, brussel sprouts and other vegetables performed better on memory tests than those who ate the fewest. Comparison of memory tests on both groups showed that women who ate their veggies scored much higher than women who didn't eat their greens. The cruciferous vegetables, those in the cabbage family, contain phytochemicals, vitamins and minerals, and fiber that are important. On other tests that measured thinking and reasoning, the women who ate their vegetables were the equivalent of one to two years younger than the women who skipped their greens.

Eating just antioxidant-rich fruits and vegetables is not enough for the brain. It also needs omega-3 and omega-6 fatty acids that are in nuts, fish, and flaxseed. The very best foods for the brain are spinach, broccoli, spirulina (blue-green algae), red apples, cranberries, blueberries, cherries, and grapes, as well as chocolate and red wine. Ideally you should have some foods from this list daily.

Nuts are perfect in-between-meal snacks. While they are high in fat and calories, it is the type of fat that protects the heart, blood vessels, and brain from plaque build-up. Another great between-meal snack is fruit or vegetable juice. Research shows that women who drank three glasses of juice a week had a much lower chance of developing Alzheimer's disease.

Remember the brain is the most important sex organ. What you feed your mind and body makes a difference in how you think and feel. Knowing what to eat can be fun. The more colorful foods are often the best and if you want to stimulate your romantic passions, chocolate ranks number one on the aphrodisiac list.

WEIGHING IN

Being the right weight is one of the best gifts you can give yourself. The *Journal of the American Medical Association* published a study showing that consuming less than 1,000 calories a day is optimal for health. For many of us that would take a lot of joy out of life. According to the Centers for Disease Control, the average man eats about 2,500 calories a day 500 more than is advised. The average woman eats 1,800 calories a day, 200 more than she needs.

Humans have evolved into an overweight, unhealthy society in part because our economic prosperity has allowed us to have plenty of food every day and that was not the situation for our ancestors. Historically food has not been in abundance and most previous generations had days with very little food available to them. Consequently, humans have evolved to store calories in the form of fat for those times where food was scarce. But now food is seldom scarce and our bodies don't have a good way to get rid of the calories we don't need, except by using our minds.

Fortunately there is plenty of room between starvation and overindulgence. One suggestion is to divide the day into 500 calorie segments. Morning, from wakeup to noon can be allotted roughly 500 calories; noon to 5 p.m. 500 more; and 5 p.m. to bedtime another 500. Most people feel better grazing than eating three major meals. If you are someone who prefers larger meals at one time of the day, dinner for instance, then subtract 100–200 calories from other

It is our choices, Harry, that show us who we really are, far more than our abilities. –J.K. Rowlings

For the Best Antioxidants, Choose Color

Best Sources of Antioxidants

Vegetables
- *Kale*
- *Spinach*
- *Brussels sprouts*
- *Alfalfa sprouts*
- *Broccoli*
- *Beets*
- *Red bell peppers*
- *Onions*

Fruits
- *Blueberries*
- *Blackberries*
- *Cranberries*
- *Strawberries*
- *Raspberries*
- *Plums*
- *Avocados*
- *Oranges*
- *Red grapes*

Berries are Brain Food—and Blues are Best!

Berries, especially blueberries, can be part of your daily diet helping both memory and motor skills.

The new food pyramid empasizes a range of foods that come from the ground, and fewer from animals.

Make your meals enjoyable by keeping them simple and "pretty."

Bounce Basics for the Mind and Body

Living ***Bounce*** means taking specific steps on a day-to-day basis to create a foundation for being your best. Being our best begins with self-awareness—knowing who you are and what you believe, awareness of others' perceptions, a commitment to growth, a confidence in your own perceptions, a realistic view of the world, and devotion to caring for yourself physically, emotionally, and spiritually. Each ***Bounce*** woman found her way through difficult times by caring for herself first, something we all found difficult, but mustered the discipline to *just do*.

The ***Bounce Basics*** are MUST DOs for the brain. They are: sleep, meditation and brain training. There is no way around these basics. *Unless the brain is working well, nothing works.* Nearly every woman I have talked to during times of distress is having difficulty in one of these areas, and before she can bounce she has to learn to control her own mind. Having control of the brain gives us the positive physical and mental health we need to live ***Bounce***. Bouncing moves us toward being our personal best, and as a result we also find happiness. Researchers now show that we can reset our happiness index through practice. For example, the more we think about and express appreciation and gratitude, the better we feel and the happier the people around us feel.

Current studies show that happy people have the best ideas, are able to see beyond themselves, care about the welfare of others, and make the greatest contributions. Nature designed us to be happy, healthy, creative, joyful, and altruistic. It is as easy to be happy as it is to be unhappy. When we think about being happy, we usually think about getting what we want, such as more money, a new car, or a different lover. But happiness doesn't come through the accumulation of things or from the love or acceptance of other people. Happiness starts in the mind.

Being happy is *not* self-indulgent. When we are in a positive state of mind, we meet our needs with minimal energy, and we move steadily toward becoming our best selves. We are able to transcend the hurdles of hassles and disappointments, skirt other people's upsets, and live joyful, productive lives that benefit others. Learn to care for your mind by prioritizing the ***Bounce Basics*** for your mind and body, and give yourself the control you need to live the life you want, being your personal best each day.

Bounce Basics create the platform for living ***Bounce*** by taking care of your brain and mind. In earlier chapters we have offered information about maintaining your hardware (the body) and your software (your thinking). In this section, our focus is on brain care.

Sleep, meditation, and brain training are brain care basics. We have a separate ***Bounce*** book titled ***Bounce Basics for the Mind and Body*** that goes into detail about the recent revelations on how the brain works, and what the brain needs in order to be fit. We want to highlight the most basic elements here because they are important. Intentionally caring for your brain is as important as caring for your body.

*There is a legend that tells of when the gods created humans.
The gods wanted to make humans like themselves, but they did not
want to make it too easy for humans to find perfection.
The gods decided they would hide one thing from
all humans: HAPPINESS! Then they decided "Let's also
give them an unquenchable desire to find it!"
They all agreed, but then one god asked "Where will we hide it?"
"We could hide it high in the mountains," suggested one god.
"No, deep in the sea," said another. Another god added,
"Oh no, that's too easy, hide it high in the sky!"
But the wisest god of all said, "We will hide it where humans
will never look. We will hide it deep within them." And so it was.
Happiness is hidden deep within the hearts
of all humankind.*

BASICS

| *Sleep* | *Meditation* | *Brain Training* |

Sleep is probably the single most important brain care basic. Sleep is listed in the hierarchy of needs in the very first and most fundamental set of core needs—those required for survival. Studies show that as many as 80% of Americans are dangerously sleep-deprived.

Many people announce with resignation, even pride, that they just don't get enough sleep, when in fact they are putting themselves and those around them at risk for accidents. Lack of sleep increases the number and seriousness of mistakes, and is the cause of irritability and fatigue. Lack of sleep becomes entangled with depression, anxiety, being overweight, headaches, colds, infection, and back pain.

The brain requires time to repair itself, resetting your internal clocks and sorting experiences into memories and developing new thoughts and ideas. The brain works nights. And if it doesn't get its work done, you are not going to get yours done either.

Meditation is the second brain care basic. Meditation is a process that takes the brain to a state of consciousness, bringing a sense of serenity, clarity, and joy. By engaging in meditation practice we can learn to manage our minds and discover new positive ways of being our best. Meditation is like a brain nap, an opportunity to take a break and return refreshed. The health benefits of meditation are difficult to study because of the complexity of the brain plus mind-body interaction. Recent studies, however, suggest that meditation benefits general health in the same ways as other emotional, spiritual, and social rituals do. Meditation helps in managing anxiety, pain, depression, mood disorders, self-esteem issues, stress, and insomnia. Symptoms from heart disease, cancer, high blood pressure, migraine headaches, and other physical problems are shown to be helped by meditation.

Brain training is brain exercise, much like exercise for the body. It is the third **Bounce Basic**. Recent scientific discoveries have changed what we know about the brain. The saying, "Can't teach an old dog new tricks," for example, is wrong, at least when applied to humans. Keeping your brain healthy and active is the *only* way to be fully engaged in life. A clear mind helps us to be present in the moment and meet our needs efficiently so we can move toward being our best. We can continue to learn and develop our minds throughout our life.

The **Bounce Basics** are about caring for the inner self rather than the outer parts of our being. We can easily slip into taking care of how we look and pay no attention to the brain and body. What happens on the inside determines both our health and happiness, while focusing on the outside often leaves us stuck and stunted.

A classic example of caring for her outer self rather that her inner self is a client named Monica. She is 35, a pretty woman with an athletic build, long reddish-blond hair, and shapely legs revealed by a short tight skirt. She has intense blue eyes and thin pastel lips, pressed together with unnatural firmness. She sits down, pulls her notebook from her purse and says, "I know change is really hard. It takes unwavering discipline, and flawless dedication." She continues, "I don't believe in therapy, but I will change, and I will do everything you say. I am ready." She makes this declaration while slamming her notebook on her lap with the vigor of a spanking, then pulls out her pen and stares expectantly at me, as though I am about to dictate the rules for her execution.

"O.K. I can help you find what you are asking for, but first," I asked, "what brought you to see me?"

Monica said, "Jamie sent me. We are life-long friends. We went to school together through college. Now, I never thought I would say this, but I want Jamie's life. Jamie has close friends, she likes her job, and she is happy in her marriage, and she is respected by other people, even her family.

"Jamie and I were like twins, superachievers, lots of boyfriends, money, beautiful clothes, everything. We both got great jobs when we graduated, but neither of us ever had a job we really liked. Our guy relationships never went past a year, and we didn't get along with our families, but we always had each other. We shared everything; we talked about all the duds we dated, our dumb bosses, and our ridiculous families.

"Then Jamie changed; she developed 'charm.' I didn't like it. She was superficial, she was always happy. She'd make syrupy compliments to real losers. I teased Jamie about losing herself in counseling. I told her she was becoming shallow and superficial.

"She wanted me to go to her shrink, but I said "Yeah, yeah, psycho-babble, it's not for me. I don't want to be brainwashed like a robot from *Stepford Wives*. That was three years ago, and I got a call from her about a year after we 'broke up' and she asked me to be in her wedding. I did it, but she was so different, we just didn't connect. I was getting focused on work, getting big promotions and raises. She just wasn't pushing herself anymore. She was volunteering somewhere, and didn't want to party anymore, so we drifted apart.

"I saw her a couple months ago and now I feel really upset. She is married and she was on her way to an award luncheon in her honor. She invited me to come along. I just had to see this, so I went. There were about 150 people and she was receiving an award for community service. When we walked into the room, she introduced me as her good friend and childhood playmate. I thought, 'Even if someone had an award luncheon for me, no one would come.' I felt tears running down my cheeks. I never cry, what is wrong with me, am I coming unglued?

"That is why I am here. I am sick of my life. I have everything, a home that was featured in the Sunday Times, designer clothes, and I know everybody important. I am ready to look at my past and examine my flaws. Whatever you say, I'll do it," she said with determination. "I can't sleep, I am a nervous wreck inside."

I said, " There is a way, but I am sorry to disappoint you. Rigorous, demanding, retrospective therapy just isn't something I practice. I think change is fun, and learning is energizing and exciting. I don't think dissecting your childhood has very much to add to your current choices."

She carefully wrote each word I said as though it were a combination of special ingredient and the secret recipe for a magic potion and she dared not miss a single word for fear the whole entire potion might be ruined.

"If you want to change, you can do it right now. Change begins the moment you choose it. To begin, tell me what is right about you. What do you like about yourself?" There was absolute silence for a few minutes before she said, "You are kidding, aren't you? Therapy is about fixing what's wrong with you, isn't it?"

I talked to Monica about the workings of her brain, and how thinking negative thoughts creates steroids and steroids ultimately leave us angry and lonely. Joy creates endorphins to heal both the mind and body and allow us to fully experience the best of ourselves. Right now your brain needs a rest and time to heal. It has been through a lot and it hasn't had time to repair itself. I explained that during sleep and meditation the neurons, the cells in the brain, have a chance to repair themselves and without that opportunity they get weak and ragged.

I asked her to get a meditation CD and put it on her iPod and start listening to it for half an hour a day. I told her the one I like is, *Your Present, A Half an Hour of Peace* by Susie Mantell, but there are many others on the Internet.

"Ooooh," Monica groaned. "I can't sleep. How on earth do you expect me to meditate?"

"Just listen to the CD, Monica, and do as she suggests. You are fighting for control of everything outside yourself and the fight is keeping you from having the peace and consciousness you need to decide what you want in life. Stop fighting and let your mind help itself." Monica was skeptical until I gave her the Chinese finger puzzle. She dutifully put both fingers in, one in each end, and pulled. As she pulled, the puzzle got tighter. "O.K., I see," she laughed. It is through caring for ourselves in everyday life that we can create the basis for being our best. The brain is *command central*; it controls our physical, emotional and spiritual health. The **Bounce Basics** of sleep, meditation and brain training give you what you need to create the life you want. Sleep and meditation give us peace of mind; being a nervous wreck is just anxiety. Anxiety is feedback from your brain that it needs more rest.

Monica found setting aside time for meditation difficult, but she had promised to do it, so she did, just before going to bed at 11:30 p.m. She didn't sleep much that night.

"I kept fighting with myself to listen," she said. "My mind would drift off in another direction so I would start the CD over. I was so frustrated, but the next night, I played it at 10:00 and thought I would get back up and watch TV afterwards. This time I remembered the Chinese finger puzzle and I quit fighting it. I just listened. My thoughts drifted off but I just kept listening. I didn't sleep any more than usual. The third night was the charm. I was listening and doing the breathing and I could feel my body letting go, then it was morning, 7 hours of sleep. I couldn't believe it."

Over the weeks that followed, Monica meditated, each night falling asleep listening to the CD. She also started developing better sleep habits since she no longer dreaded going to bed. In less than a month, she announced in disbelief, "I'm not nervous anymore. I go to bed at 10:30 every night and get up at 6:00 a.m. I feel good every day."

Establishing healthy sleep rituals is important, and putting sleep at the top of your to do list is a good idea.

Sleep—A *Bounce Basic*

Sleep means to rest from normal body and brain activity. Sleep is in the first category of core needs and is essential for brain and body health. While you are sleeping, your brain is busy. Sleep helps the nervous system work properly. It strengthens the immune system, keeping the body safe from infection. Complete sleep improves memory, enhances physical and athletic performance abilities, and gives us emotional stability and resilience. Sleep gives neurons a chance to shut down and repair themselves. Without sleep, neurons lose their energy and become dysfunctional. Sleep gives the brain a chance to repair neural networks.

Chemical messenger hormones like serotonin and norepinephrine control sleep. There are five stages of sleep that occur nightly, making a complete sleep cycle: stages 1, 2, 3, 4, and REM (rapid eye movement) sleep. We move from one stage to another; then the cycle starts over. Completing all five stages of the cycle is important to physical and mental health.

Stage 1 is light sleep, a stage from which we can easily wake up; 2 is the stage where our brain waves change from our most active (beta waves) to slower (theta waves); stage 3 is a transitional stage with brain waves becoming slower and slower. Deep sleep is stage 4 and is predominantly delta waves—the slowest of our brain waves.

Deep sleep is the stage that helps us maintain our emotional balance. When we talk about someone's nerves being frayed, or they are cranky because they didn't get enough sleep, it is because of the lack of stage 4 deep sleep. When stage 4 sleep is disrupted or we don't get enough, decision-making, perception, math skills, reasoning, and memory are all affected.

The final sleep stage is REM—Rapid Eye Movement—sleep, so named because the eyes move around, breathing becomes more rapid and irregular, arms and legs become temporarily paralyzed. The heart rate increases and blood pressure rises. REM sleep begins about 60 to 90 minutes into the sleep cycle. The first REM sleep happens about an hour after we fall asleep. REM sleep affects learning, memory, and comprehension.

Five Sleep Stages

1. Light sleep—drifting in and out of sleep; eye and muscle movements slow
2. Eye movement stops; brain waves slow
3. The brain slows and delta waves dominate brain wave activity
4. Deep sleep, slow delta waves, no eye or muscle movement
5. REM sleep; bodily changes occur. Breathing becomes irregular and arms and legs become temporarily paralyzed.

A complete sleep cycle takes an hour and a half to two hours. The beginning sleep cycles each night contain relatively short REM periods and long periods of deep sleep. As the night progresses, REM sleep periods increase in length while deep sleep decreases. We spend around 2 hours a night dreaming. REM is the dreamer's sleep, and REM sleep is so important that if REM sleep is disrupted one night, our bodies go directly into REM sleep and stay in REM longer than usual to "catch up."

The first half of the night is spent mostly in stages 1 and 3; during the second half of the night REM stages occur more and more frequently. Sleep is affected by food, medications, chemicals, and temperature. Caffeinated drinks such as coffee and drugs such as diet pills or decongestants interfere with sleep cycles. Antidepressants can disrupt REM sleep. Smoking impacts sleep in several ways. It limits the amount of REM sleep causing the smoker to sleep lightly and wake easily. Smokers also wake up more often because the brain experiences nicotine withdrawal during the night. Sleeping in a room that is too hot or too cold also disrupts REM sleep because the body cannot regulate its temperature.

A nightcap causes more sleep problems than it solves. Alcohol disrupts REM sleep. The brain experiences alcohol withdrawal, just as it does with nicotine, making sleep lighter, with frequent waking during the night. This may be one factor in why smokers and drinkers look older than they actually are.

One of the women from the **Bounce** Circle, Kathy, admitted she had not slept for more than three or four hours at a time for the past 10 years since her divorce. Kathy told the Circle, "I have tried everything, so I have just come to accept it. I feel better if I can take a nap, but since I work all day, naps seldom happen." Sandra commented, "I had trouble sleeping for years, until I went to the sleep clinic. I was diagnosed with sleep apnea. Have you gone to a sleep clinic?"

"No, I haven't," Kathy replied, "sleep clinics are expensive and I don't have sleep apnea. I don't snore." Sandra added, "I felt like a different person once I started sleeping well. I use a CPAP machine and my life sure works better when I am not on the edge all day." By the end of the evening Kathy changed her goal and moved sleep to the top of her list and decided to try once more to solve her sleep problem.

At our last Circle meeting, Kathy had been to the sleep clinic for a sleep study, and as she thought, she did not have sleep apnea, but she was officially diagnosed as sleep-deprived, and a program was created for her to retrain her brain for sleeping. At the time of our last meeting she was sleeping six hours straight, the longest she had slept in years. She expects to be up to eight hours in another month. She says, "I knew it would make a difference if I could sleep all night, but I had no idea how crummy I felt until now. Even with just six hours a night I feel more energetic than I have in years."

Kathy isn't alone in not being able to sleep. Sadly, nearly 80% of Americans have some level of sleep deprivation, making it impossible for them to be their best. Annually 100,000 auto accidents are caused by sleepiness, resulting in an average of 1,500 deaths.

The amount of sleep we need varies between individuals. According to studies people who sleep between 6.5 hrs and 7.5 hrs a night live the longest. People who sleep more than 8 hrs or less than 6.5 hrs hour die at a younger age. Sleeping too much or too little is life-threatening.

Babies need about 16 hours of sleep a day, while teenagers need about 9 hours on average. Adults usually need 7 to 8 hours a night although the usual range is around 6 to 9 hours. People over 65 may need less sleep than they did when they were younger.

The amount of sleep we need is so crucial that the brain and body demand that we keep it up. When we don't get enough sleep one night, we should make it up as soon as possible. It is called sleep debt: If you don't get through all your sleep cycles, you owe a debt. And your mind and body insist it be repaid. The amount of sleep needed the night after a sleepless night increases. We don't get used to less sleep. Whatever the amount of sleep a person needs, that amount continues as a need until it is met. Like credit-card debt, sleep debt grows until it is repaid.

You are not getting enough sleep if you:
- feel tired or sleepy
- hit bottom about 4 p.m.
- use the snooze alarm
- have trouble going to sleep
- need more than 20 minutes to get to sleep
- fall asleep when your head hits the pillow
- don't want to get up in the morning
- are clumsy
- wake up more than once during the night
- have difficulty making decisions

Another individual difference is between those who wake up early in the morning ready to go (doves) and those who wake slowly and stay up late at night (owls). The doves have measurably higher levels of a steroid hormone, corticol, in the mornings than owls.

Psychologist Dr. Angela Clow from the University of Westminster, England, reports from her study, "Early awakening has been associated with greater powers of concentration, being busier and experiencing more hassles through the day, as well as having more anger and less energy at the end of the day.

"On the other hand, late wakers were more leisurely and less busy. It is possible the cortisol may contribute towards these differences in temperament because it is known to influence mood and concentration," she said.

Interestingly, the doves had more colds, muscle aches, headaches, and moodiness than owls. The *British Medical Journal* reported a study involving over 1,200 men and women over a 25-year period. The research found that owls who slept in were just as healthy and a little more wealthy than doves. In reality whether you are a dove or an owl sleeper doesn't make much difference, but getting *enough* sleep does.

Sleep medication is prescribed to tens of millions of people every year and more than half of the people who take these medications experience significant side affects. There are sleep tools that are better than prescription medication. One of the most effective tools according to *Web*MD is a sound machine—a machine that plays either white noise or your choice of soothing sounds such as a running brook or a soft rainfall. Over-the-counter medications come in second on *Web*MD's list of effective treatments, followed by consistent bedtime routines, meditation or muscle relaxation, and a new mattress.

Nightly, complete sleep cycles are basic to being our best. To perform well, concentrate, have optimum memory, good emotional control and **Bounce**, a complete night's sleep is a must. If you have trouble sleeping, it is a problem that must be solved. For sweet dreams, sleep with fresh flowers in your room. Sleep is a **Bounce** Basic.

SLEEP TIPS

1. Create a quiet cool environment for sleep and sex only! No computer, no TV, no phone, no pda, nothing. A bedroom is a place to sleep. It is O.K. to read, if the book is boring!

2. A cool room temperature is optimal, using blankets for warmth rather than heating the air. A drop in body temperature signals the brain that it is time to shut down.

3. Go to bed at the same time every night. Create some routines around going to bed: washing your face, brushing your teeth, drinking a cup of herbal tea, listening to soft music, meditating or doing some deep breathing.

4. Have a glass of milk, some yogurt, or cheese before bed if you are hungry. Preferably half an hour before bedtime.

5. If you like to take a bath to relax before going to bed, do it an hour and a half before bedtime. Raising your body temperature can make it harder to sleep.

If you have trouble sleeping . . .
- do not drink caffeine after noon.
- be sure you finish exercising 4 hours before bedtime.
- use ear plugs or a white noise machine.
- wear a sleep mask or eye covers.
- do not take naps.
- if you are not asleep in 20 minutes, get up and do something boring, do not watch TV.
- do not go to bed until you are sleepy.
- open the shades and let the sun/light in when you wake up. Light signals the brain to wake up.
- do not drink alcohol.
- get a new mattress if yours is more than 10 years old.

Sleep apnea is a common and serious sleep disorder. It happens when a person stops breathing for 10 seconds or more while asleep. Sleep is interrupted and normal sleep cycles are disrupted. Symptoms of sleep apnea are snoring, a coughing or choking sound during the night, waking up feeling out of breath and morning headaches.

During daytime people with sleep apnea feel tired or groggy, like they just are not fully awake. Sleep apnea leads to moodiness that can be thought of as depression or anxiety. More seriously, even deadly, sleep apnea can contribute to high blood pressure, stroke, irregular heartbeat, and nighttime heart attacks. The good news is that sleep apnea is successfully treated.

Many times simple sleep hygiene takes care of the problem. Avoid alcohol and sleeping pills; elevate the head of your bed by 4 to 6 inches (bed risers are commercially available); change your sleeping posture (avoid sleeping on your back); don't smoke; and lose weight if you are 25 pounds or more overweight.

Continuous positive airway pressure (CPAP) is also an effective treatment. A mask is worn over the mouth and nose at night. The mask is hooked up to a machine that pushes continuous streams of air into the mask keeping the airways open.

There are other successful treatments, also. Dentists can make devices that help keep the airway open during sleep. And doctors can perform surgery if there is a defect in the nose, tonsils or jaw. Whatever the cause of the problem, sleep apnea can and should be solved. It is, as they say, "not compatible with life."

Sleep medication is prescribed to tens of millions of people every year and more than half of the people who take these medications experience significant side effects.

Meditation—A *Bounce Basic*

Many beliefs about the brain have been discovered to be false thanks to recent scientific advances. For many years people thought that we used only part of the brain. Not true, we use every single cell. It has been thought that over time we lose brain cells through aging, injury, drug or alcohol use, and once they are gone, that is it. Not true, scientists now say. The brain continues to produce new brain cells well into our 80s and perhaps beyond.

It turns out that the brain is highly adaptive, conforming to our needs. This ability to transform itself is called neuroplasticity. "Neuro" refers to cells in the brain and "plasticity" means the ability to change form or structure, meaning the brain has the ability to change itself.

Neuroplasticity means the brain behaves in the same way as muscles—the more we use them, the stronger they become. It also means when they are not used, they shrink. The brain expands in the areas we use and prunes the areas we don't. Recently studies have recommended that we can ward off Alzheimer's disease by learning new things as we get older, rather than doing the same old things.

According to a recent book, *Train Your Mind, Change Your Brain*, the brain is highly adaptive and flexible. An early proponent of exploring neuroplasticity is Tibet's spiritual leader, the Dalai Lama, who believes there is harmony between science and religion. He regularly invites groups of scientists to his home in Dharamsala, India.

At one of the Dalai Lama's creative retreats, he was told that the mind can change the body. He questioned could the mind change the brain? Could what you think change your brain chemistry; could it change brain circuits or even the brain's structure?

Following several years of discussion, the Dalai Lama asked some of his followers, monks who meditate daily, to agree to have their brains scanned to determine if the brain actually changed because of meditation. Many of these monks have meditated for over 10,000 hours, focusing on loving kindness, wishing for the happiness of others, and for universal relief from suffering. Their agreement to participate in a scientific study led to breakthroughs in understanding the brain and the mind. (The mind is what the brain does.) The study found that compassionate meditation changes the brain. Professor Richard Davidson after studying the evidence writes, "This positive state (compassion) is a skill that can be trained and that training changes the function of the brain in an enduring way." *Compassion means showing feelings of sympathy and caring for the suffering of others, usually with a desire to help.*

Compassion means showing feelings of sympathy for the suffering of others, often with a desire to help. Compassionate meditation focuses on people in general not a specific person.

We have the ability to intentionally and deliberately change our minds, becoming more empathetic toward others. And in so doing we become happier and healthier, since self-awareness and self-acceptance are the first steps in becoming our personal best. Dr. Davidson says we can take advantage of our brain's plasticity and train ourselves to be more kind and compassionate. "Thinking about other people's suffering and not just your own helps to put everything in perspective," he says, adding that "learning compassion for oneself is a critical first step." He adds, "Compassionate meditation can be beneficial in promoting more harmonious relationships of all kinds."

Meditation changes your mind. Taking care of your mind is an important step in creating a kind and compassionate world within and around you.

The Dalai Lama holds regular spiritual, artistic, and scientific discussions in his home in exile in Dharamsala, India. It is located in the northern Indian state of Himachal Pradesh. It is on the Dhauladhar range of the Himalayas.

THE MAGIC OF MEDITATION

Meditation isn't really magic, although it sure seemed like it to me. I always try to be sure I can do what I recommend to others, so I tried meditation after I read an article in TIME magazine entitled, *Calming the Mind.* For me, it was . . . magical. After about a month of meditating, listening to an audio CD, *Your Present: A Half Hour of Peace,* by Susie Mantell, I began sleeping longer and more easily than I have in my entire life. Now I find it easy to quiet my mind whenever I want.

Most types of meditation have five elements in common:

1. A quiet location; a quiet place with as few distractions as possible.
2. A comfortable posture. Meditation can be done while sitting, lying down, standing, walking, or in other positions.
3. Focus. Focusing your attention is usually a part of meditation. Some people use a mantra like Ohm, some choose an object, and others focus on their breathing.
4. An open mind. Being open-minded means letting distractions come and go naturally without stopping to think about them. When distracting or wandering thoughts occur, the meditator gently brings attention back to the focus.
5. Observation. Some meditators simply observe their thoughts and emotions without responding.

BRAIN WAVES—ALPHA, BETA, DELTA AND THETA

All humans have the same brain waves, irrespective of culture, race, gender, or age. Brain waves are categorized as alpha, beta, delta and theta. Alpha brain waves are present when we are calm, quiet and relaxed. It is alpha waves that we are seeking during meditation. They give the brain a break. Like with all brain activities too much and too little are both bad. Too many alpha waves leaves a person feeling like they are comatose. There is a high level of alpha waves present when we watch TV.

Beta waves are present when we are fully alert and engaged. They are the fastest and most intense of all the brain waves. Concentrating, studying, or being actively involved in conversation all produce beta waves. Too much beta is a racing mind and inability to focus.

Delta waves take place when we are in deep sleep. Sleep occurs in 90-minute cycles and during these cycles the neurons repair themselves and the brain organizes information and experiences. Delta waves are present in REM sleep when we are dreaming and in deep, dreamless sleep.

Theta waves give us a sense of daydreaming. They usually occur when we are doing something routine, so we have some beta wave activity but are not really paying attention. Theta waves can happen while we're taking a shower, running, or freeway driving. Many people experience a flood of creativity or problem-solving ideas during theta waves.

So take a look at the difference in the brain before meditation and after. Most of the women I know have trouble quieting their minds, and meditation really does work. *Functional Magnetic Resonance Imaging (fmri) is an imaging process that visually shows activity while the brain is working.*

Before and After Meditation

Reds, pinks and yellows are beta waves.
Blues are alpha and theta waves.

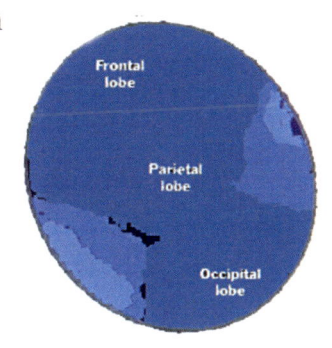

These are fmri images of the brain taken before a person was taught meditation (left). The second fmri image (right) was taken after one session of meditation. The differences in the brain's activity before and after meditation is profound, showing the reduction in beta waves in the cortex of the brain. It is the cortex that processes information, so when you have a lot on your mind, give your brain a quick nap and it will be more alert and more efficient afterward.

Images from a Time magazine article based on the book, The Ancesteral Mind.

In just half an hour yoga can boost gray matter, to improve memory, and give you endorphins.

Yoga—A Bounce Basic

- Lowers high blood pressure.
- Relieves depression.
- Improves chronic low back pain.
- Reduces or eliminates fatigue.
- Reduces the intensity and frequency of tension or migraine headaches, decreasing use of pain-relieving drugs.
- Improves sleep efficiency, quality of sleep.
- Reduces irritable bowel syndrome (IBS).
- Improves memory.
- Helps treat anxiety disorders, obsessive-compulsive disorders, and schizophrenia.
- Improves asthma, especially with breathing exercises.

Brain Training—A *Bounce Basic*

Brain training means taking care of your brain's health. Like the body, the brain needs exercise in the form of lifelong learning, positive thinking, experiencing new events, having surprises, and playing mind games. Our little three-pound brain, with 60% fat, has more than a hundred trillion connections—each able to make 200 calculations per second. WOW!

The brain needs stimulation. In fact, it loves surprises! When the brain is surprised, it really lights up, according to brain scientists. Brain experts say that active learning throughout life helps maintain brain health, and if it seems to the brain as if we don't need it, snip-snip, there it goes.

As we age, the brain can get lazy. If we only do what we have done before—watch TV, listen to music, clean the house, tend the garden, drive the usual routes, and so forth—the brain slows down and conserves energy, which means it is half asleep.

The brain gets busy building new neural pathways when we learn new skills, acquire a new ability, engage in a new activity, or discover a new interest. Our neural networks reorganize and repair themselves according to our experiences. These experiences can be physical actions by the body or mental actions of the brain. Neurons connect with muscles, as well as with other neurons. The brain and body cross-stimulate; as the body changes so does the brain. This is why physical exercise is essential for brain health.

The physical exercise that most benefits the brain is walking. Unlike other more aerobic exercises, the muscles don't use up the body's oxygen and nutrients. Walking increases the size of the blood vessels in the brain as well as the heart rate, allowing more oxygen to get to the brain and more toxins to be removed. A recent study showed that walking just 20 minutes a day improves learning ability, concentration, and abstract reasoning. Stroke risk was cut in half. Women who walked less than half a mile per week lost brain function, simply due to aging, but women who walked even a mile a week retained their sharpness longer. If a five-minute walk is what you can do, do it. Every little bit helps.

Intentionally caring for the brain is simple, in fact, it is fun, and takes very little time. Considering the benefits of keeping your brain healthy it is well worth the effort. In addition to the benefits of physical exercise, the brain thrives on mental exercises. We call them mind games.

Connection with other people is stimulating to the brain. When you think about it, nothing is more surprising than people. Making connections with others can be as simple as a "Hello" with a smile, or as complicated as an emotional conversation. One of the very best ways to train the brain is dancing! You make a connection with a partner, you remember the steps and you move. Three for one! And, if you laugh you get even more benefits. Have fun training your brain.

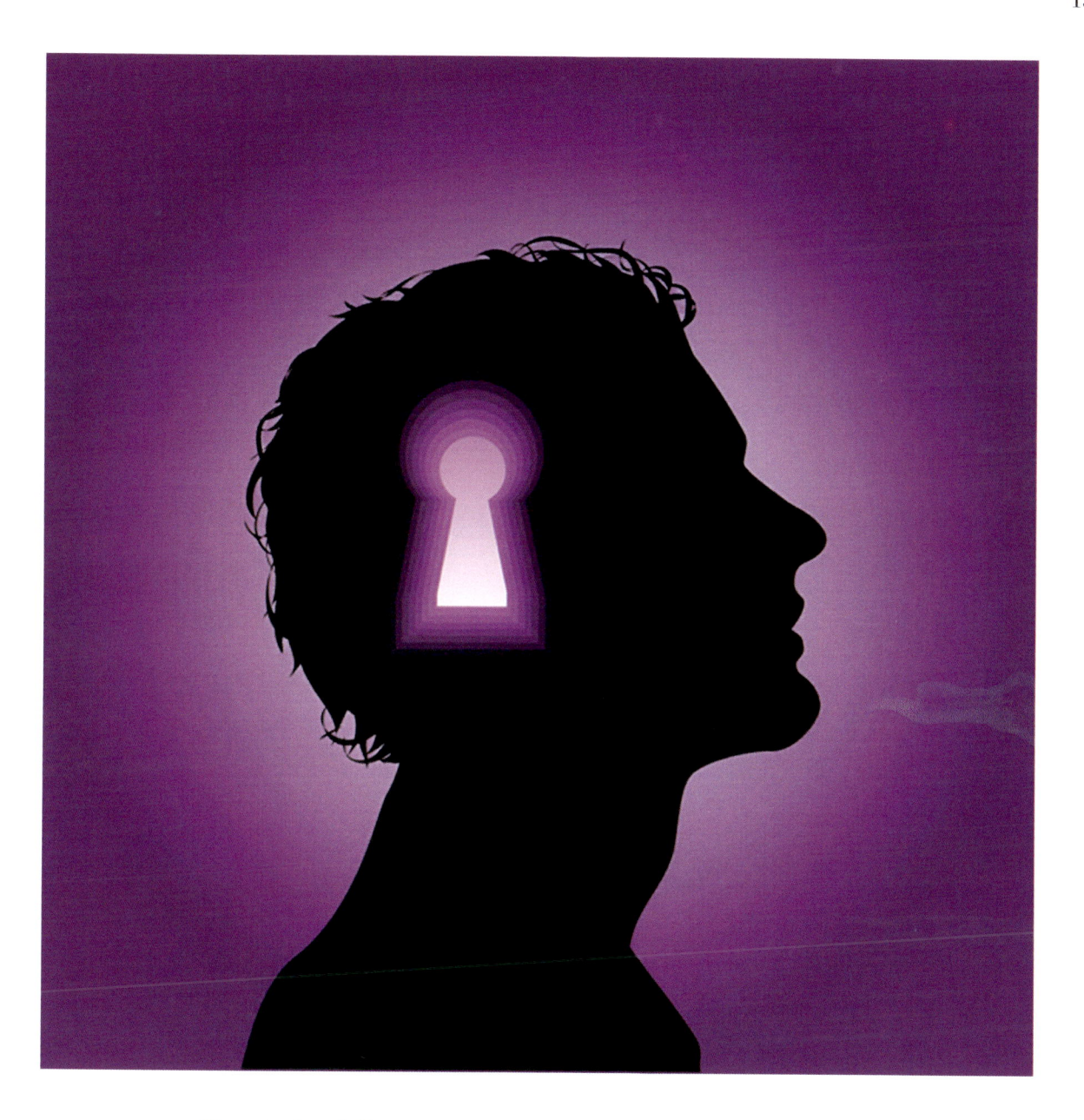

*The mind is different from the brain. The mind is the combined
effort of various brain activities in concert with the workings of the body.
Too complicated? Basically the mind is what the brain does. Mental health is
evidence of how the mind and body are doing. Training the brain is the key
to keeping your mind and body healthy and lively.*

Growing up, I lived across the field from my grandparents and they were a joyful part of my childhood. My grandmother allowed me to do things my mother would not, like soaking my cookies in my milk, and drinking coffee (albeit mostly milk). I made many treks across the field and the path became very well-worn. When I thought my mother was really out of line, I knew exactly where I was going. Every time I ran away from home, I went straight for the path. Neural pathways are the same—the more we use them the more automatic and efficient they become. But there is a down side. Because they are so automatic, we often believe that what we think about ourselves is right when, in truth, it is nothing more than a well-worn path. After going over the same route the connections begin to store information, and that stored information becomes memory.

The human brain is made up of hundreds of billions of cells called neurons. Each neuron is connected to other neurons forming neural connections. These neural connections form neural pathways that weave their way throughout the brain creating something like a superhighway.

Electrical charges run through these neural pathways releasing chemical messengers, neurotransmitters, like endorphins and steroids. These neurotransmitters communicate with the body. The more frequently the same neural pathways are used, the more efficient they become.

All we have to do to be different than we have been is to create new neural paths, and we do that by being intentional in our thinking. We have the ability to think new thoughts, and each time we do, the brain changes a little, and over time the new pathways take over. Something as simple as slowly moving your toes when you wake up and before you get up, activates neurons that stimulate both the brain and the body.

It is true of all of us that our willingness to challenge our own thinking allows us strength and adaptability that makes our lives more joyful and fulfilling. The brain literally lights up according to fmri's when we think new thoughts. Simply reconsidering your thoughts adds to your ability to bounce.

Keeping your brain fit is one of the best insurances you can get for coping well with whatever comes along, whether it is joyful or difficult. Living life at your 90%+ level takes only a little effort and adds years of joy to life.

Individual neuron

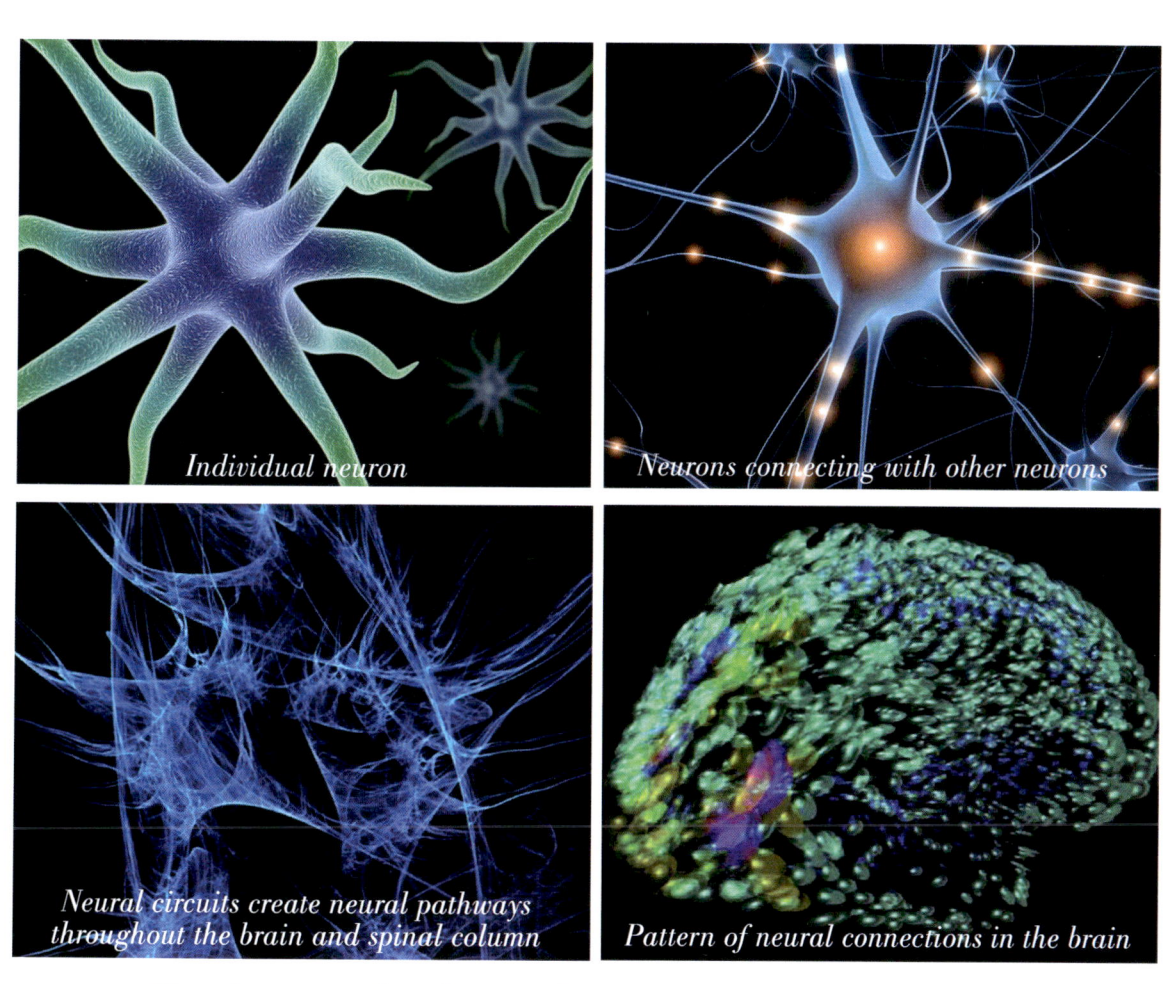

Neurons connecting with other neurons

Neural circuits create neural pathways throughout the brain and spinal column

Pattern of neural connections in the brain

These images are from functional magnetic resonance imaging (fmri).

MIND GAMES

Patricia, our neighbor, has been a consistent reader of multiple drafts of this book over the past couple of years, so many days went into evening talking about **Bounce**. Once my editor, Judy, arrived in August, the three of us started putting in long hours of writing and editing this **Bounce, Be Transformed** book. One aspect of the **Bounce** women is that we really try what we recommend, so we decided to play. I already did Sudoku and crossword puzzles, so I bought a game of Scrabble. We now bounce through our Scrabble game night with pure joy and hilarity, inventing words that no one on earth would recognize, intermixed with the normal English language of course. One reason we like Scrabble is that winning or losing is largely the luck of your draw, not your intellect. We also like Left, Right, Center—a dice game—for the same reason. It is just pure luck, and luck changes—giving the brain the surprise.

In our **Bounce** Circle, we asked the women to set aside one hour a week for simple play. Play means doing something just for the *fun* of it, with no other value or meaning. All but two people out of 12 in our group had trouble finding pure play activities. Have some fun playing mind games with yourself or friends! Do something different just for the sake of doing it differently. Here are some ideas:

Try using your nondominant hand to eat a meal. That will certainly come as a surprise to your brain. Brush your teeth, comb your hair, move the computer mouse, put away the dishes all with the "other" hand.

Dancing is one of the best brain exercises because your body is busy. Your brain is working to remember the steps and you are making a social connection all at the same time.

Think about your breathing; is it fast or slow, easy or difficult, deep or shallow? Is your chest moving? Is your diaphragm pushing? It gives your brain a little extra oxygen.

Go to the kids' toy department at the drugstore and get some modeling clay, then sculpt your clay while you listen to music. Do sudoku or crossword puzzles.

Play cards: bridge, poker, pinochle, rummy, hearts or, if necessary, solitaire.

Play chess.

Do tai chi.

Take a trip and tell about it or write about it.

Play Scrabble, Pictionary, Monopoly, Checkers, or Trivial Pursuit.

Bounce women Scrabble!

Pleasure Your Brain—with People

It seems like every study I have read on health and happiness ends up making the point that relationships with other people are important to our physical and mental health. Shopping, going out to dinner, playing tennis, going to a movie with a friend, are all good for your brain because they involve social interaction. Even a simple conversation with a checker at the grocery store or a phone call to a relative improves your mind. Any *positive* interaction with another person or pet reduces the effects of stress and aging on the brain.

A major public-health study involving more than 116,000 participants found that people with strong relationships had less mental decline and lived more active, pain-free lives, without physical limitations.

Other studies suggest that people with the most limited social connections are twice as likely to die over a given period than more articulate people. Even better, those who continue to learn new things stay sharper longer.

Sometimes after a crisis it is tempting to withdraw and be by yourself. But, if you want to **Bounce**, you have to connect. The brain likes stimulation and surprise and nothing is as surprising as people. Just do something where you have contact with others, even if it is superficial. It is best to have contact at least twice a week with someone you care about who cares about you. Consider these ideas:

1. Pursue social activities, like political events, lecture programs, or traveling with friends.
2. Go to events on a regular basis. For instance, take a class, attend church, join a club, organize a weekly card game with neighbors.
3. Volunteer for a cause even if you are not that excited about it at first. If nothing else you have a new experience and that is a good thing.
4. Join the museum and go to their events and shows.
5. Get involved with a charity
6. Join a health club and sign up for group activities, like a biking club, hiking group, or yoga class—or learn to play golf.
7. Get yourself a pet. Pets are a great source of companionship and pleasure, and scientists have shown that owning a pet lowers blood pressure, reduces signs of stress, and helps us feel connected. Just be sure your pet doesn't become a reason to stay home. If you have a dog and take it for walks that is a sure-fire way to meet neighbors. When I walk our dog, Noir, I almost always end up talking to someone, even if it is only to say, "Good morning."

We do not all have the same level of need for social contact. It is not necessary to become an extrovert if you are an introvert. Just give yourself a little nudge to say "hello," smile and wish someone a "good day."

One amazing study from the Cleveland Clinic Foundation showed that a muscle can be strengthened just by thinking about exercising it. Over the course of four months one study group concentrated on exercising either their little finger or their elbow for five minutes a day, five days a week. *All movements were imaginary.* Another comparable study group did nothing. The muscle strength in the little finger from imaginary exercise increased 35% and the elbow strength went up 13%, while the comparable group that did not nothing showed no change. Remember—all the exercise was in the mind only! Brain scans taken after the study showed greater and more focused activity in the prefrontal cortex than before. The researchers said strength gains were due to improvements in the brain's ability to signal muscle.

What we think and how we focus the brain changes our lives and our minds. As a child I remember reading and rereading *The Little Engine that Could,* and the power of the words, "I think I can. I think I can." I now appreciate how important learning positive thinking is for our brain health. When we think we are unable, we *are* unable. And, when we think we are able, we are. Challenging our beliefs is part of **Bounce**. Having new experiences for the sake of having new experiences is essential in training your brain.

Our **Bounce** Circle has started our own monthly play dates for brain exercise, and having fun at the same time. Once a month we go out together to do something we haven't done before. We have been to the horse races, a baseball game, a Beach Boys concert, a picnic in the park, a boat ride, and we are going to the women's body-building event with Susan. We have fun and it gives our brains a new experience, a surprise and some exercise. Plus we get some endorphins from being together seeking joy.

In addition to having fun together, we find that talking through issues and decisions is always useful. The influence of other women who believe in growth and transformation has allowed us as well as many of the women in other **Bounce** Circles to avoid making costly decisions especially during an emotionally difficult time.

During times of intense upset, the brain has difficulty focusing clearly and rationally. When women are in fear mode—fight, flight, freeze or surrender—our brain speeds up, searching every possible nook and cranny for solutions. Unlike the male brain that slows down and focuses on one or two areas of thought, the female brain goes faster.

It is tempting to want to end the chaos and angst by ending the source of the pain. Stopping the pain by ending a relationship, quitting a job or moving away from the source, can do more harm than good. Keeping your brain in balance while moving forward helps the most. One of the main ground rules in our **Bounce** Circles is focusing on what to do now. Not the past or the future. We spend time and energy helping each other figure out what we really want, based on identifying and meeting our core needs *while emphasizing our **Bounce** Basics—sleep, meditation and brain training.*

Women have millions of billions of interneural connections in the brain, and we can draw from many parts of the brain all at the same time. Calming the mind and soothing the body are essential aspects of making good decisions. Other women who are listening and thinking about how you can meet your needs, rather than through judgment or the lens of right or wrong, can give you the perspective you need to navigate through troubled times.

Claudia is a good example of someone whose life was moving along pleasantly when her husband dropped the proverbial bombshell. Claudia was a member of one of our **Bounce** Circles. A short time after our first Circle meeting, Claudia discovered her husband was having an affair. "We stopped having sex five years ago, or maybe longer," Claudia sighed. "I was willing, but he just didn't seem interested. Sex had never been a big part of our marriage, but I had asked him if he was seeing someone else, and he always said, "If I felt like having sex, it would be with you; I think I am just getting old."

"I believed him," she told us, "until I found a card in his briefcase signed, 'I will always love you. –Georgia.' My eyes filled with tears. I was surprised by the heaviness in my heart. When he came home from work and I told him I knew about his affairs. I didn't know, but I thought I could trap him that way. He said he had two affairs." Claudia told him she wanted a divorce. He said, "O.K."

She continued, "He lied and cheated. I am going to sell our house, use the money to buy a house in the country, and have a garden and dogs. I'll get a small condo in the city for when I am in town. Who knows a good lawyer?" she asked.

"Are you sure you want to be single?" another person asked. Claudia nodded, "Yes". She was sure she wanted a divorce. Someone gave Claudia the name of a lawyer—it is always good to know the rules before you play the game. We suggested Claudia also see a divorce accounting specialist who would figure out what the dollar amount really means going forward. We also suggested she list the needs that were currently being met by being married, since she still had one son at home and a daughter starting college. We also cautioned her not to tell her friends and extended family, just yet. She agreed.

At our next **Bounce** Circle, Claudia told us about her meeting with the accounting specialist. Frank had said he didn't care about the money; she could have it. She found out from the financial advisor that although she would probably get a substantial settlement, she still would have to cut her lifestyle by 40%–50%. The advisor also cautioned her that Frank probably wouldn't continue to earn as much as he had in the past since he didn't enjoy his work and he didn't care about money. If Frank gave her most of the money, she would probably be the one paying for the kids' college. She would not be able to afford a country house and a city condo and have money to live on. In fact, she would not even be able to keep the house she has now. Claudia was stunned, but insisted "I won't stay married to a liar and cheat."

Someone in the Circle asked, "If you don't want to be married, do you want to be single? I know you are hurt and disappointed, but you said that before you found out about the affair that you were mostly happy and you never considered a divorce, so why get a divorce now when that isn't what you wanted before?" Claudia whispered, "I didn't want a divorce, but I never thought he would lie and cheat."

"I just can't stand the thought that I was so stupid and he lied. Then when I confronted him, I thought he would be so sorry and beg for my forgiveness, but he didn't. He just said he didn't want to live this way anymore. He says the way we live is too extravagant and wasteful. I was dumbfounded. I thought he loved our home. He says it isn't his home, it is my home, it is just a house to him."

"I am not going to lower my lifestyle because he is having a mid-life crisis. I won't live on the cheap. I won't," she said emphatically. Claudia knew what she *didn't* want, but not what she did, but she thought she had to decide something and do something, now. We encouraged her to just give herself some time and not make choices until she recovered from some of the shock and trauma of confronting the loss of her beliefs about their marriage.

Never rush toward something you don't want. It just doesn't turn out well. As hard as it is to know what we *do* want, it is worth taking the time. Even when it means doing nothing while you are in pain or suffering. Doing something to teach someone else a lesson or to try to end your pain usually backfires. It is usually you who learns the lesson, and it doesn't change the pain. The pain will run its course, like all emotions. Fear, anger, sadness, disgust, and joy—all our core emotions have a normal cycle, so just let them flow. It may seem like they won't end, but they will.

Never rush toward something you don't want.

Deciding what we want is difficult, anytime, but especially during a time of crisis. Claudia's distress at having been fooled, and the fear of losing her lifestyle can take her toward exactly the outcome she didn't want. If she holds on to her belief that she is stupid for believing Frank, she will feel bad and have lower self-esteem, thinking she is a victim.

If she proceeds down the divorce path, she cannot possibly maintain her current lifestyle. If she stays with Frank, she can't have the same lifestyle either. But instead of acting in fear, taking time lets them both recover and rethink their options.

When Claudia decided to step back and treat the crisis in their marriage as a *rough spot*, she stopped herself from speeding toward a divorce she didn't want. Transitions and transformation do not occur without loss, but fear of loss is not a good reason to stop moving toward figuring out what you want. Nor is it a good idea to throw caution to the wind and just *go for it* without regard to consequences.

Claudia and Frank have been living their married life on her terms for 20 years, maybe a change could be good. It is at least worth finding out. Insisting on *musts* and *can'ts* is silly and self-limiting. Claudia's change in thinking from reacting with moral indignation to a more pragmatic approach, deciding what is important to her at this next stage of her life, changes the direction of her life, giving her more time and clarity to make a decision of this magnitude.

It is sometimes easy to default to a way we thought at another time in our lives or it may be religious or cultural values that allow us to believe in an absolute right or wrong. Claudia always thought if *her* husband ever had an affair, he would be *out the door*. Most women think they would throw *him* out or *get even* if their husband had an affair, but that isn't what we do. In fact, most women do the opposite; they work harder on their marriage. They change their minds and their lives. And, hopefully, they bounce toward making themselves stronger and happier and don't become a slave to the marriage.

Fear is like a flashing yellow light; slow down; look around. Move ahead.

Women seem to easily claim their fears. "I can't" or "I don't" or "I couldn't" rolls off the tongues of perfectly able women. These absolutes we create in our minds are just fears. If we turn our fears into righteous thinking, we become stuck and blocked from our own growth and chances for transformation. Fear is not a red light that means stop and stay where you are. Fears simply warn us, like a flashing yellow light. Slow down, look around and proceed cautiously ahead.

While Claudia thought she knew what she would do if Frank ever had an affair, she decided to rethink her absolutes. All of them, not just about Frank. Maybe she didn't need a lifestyle this lavish, but if she gave that up, how would she meet the needs that lifestyle had met? Another question she began to ask herself was whether their big beautiful house was really meeting her needs. "Maybe it is time for updating my thinking," she concluded. "I am entering a new time in my life with or without Frank. I don't know what I want, so I will have to try some new thinking."

Life happens—unexpectedly sometimes. Staying healthy in mind and body is the best way to be prepared for whatever comes your way. The higher the level you start at, the better you bounce. The **Bounce Basics** focus on your brain, since it is command central for both mind and body. Beyond the **Bounce Basics**, we have created the **Bounce Essentials**.

The **Bounce Essentials** are designed to keep your endorphin levels high. We have tested the **Basics** and **Essentials** on ourselves and in the **Bounce** Circles. They work. Plus, they are easy to incorporate into real lives to keep bouncing. We have an acronym for the **Bounce Essentials**—MENTAL.

The ABCs of MENTAL

Endorphins are truly miraculous, keeping us healthy and happy, able to live our lives at the 90%+ level, plus they are always available and free. The **Bounce** women are intentional about creating endorphins on a daily basis. We have found that developing routines help keep us on track with maintaining our endorphin levels.

We have six ways to make endorphins part of our daily routine and they form the acronym **MENTAL**.

M = Move
E = Experience
N = Nourish
T = Touch
A = Appreciate
L = Laugh

There are other ways to help yourself keep your endorphin levels high. These are a few ideas that have worked for us. By routinely keeping our endorphin levels high, we fuel the brain, mind and body. The pages in the MENTAL section of this book are colorful pictures to give you inspiration for all the activities—physical and emotional—that you can weave into your life.

The MENTAL steps also allow you to create a positive environment around yourself. It is difficult to create endorphins in yourself if the world around you is a mess. Each of the **Bounce** women has found that by being conscious of our own needs, we become more patient and positive with others. We are deliberate in looking for the good in others, assuming the best, and being quick to forgive. A simple compliment, a generous smile, or a loving touch does wonders for ourselves and those around us.

Caring for ourselves first allows us to be fulfilled and joyful. I believe that it is because we maintain a high level of self-awareness that we can avoid absorbing the issues or upsets of others. **Bounce** has also given us tools that help change the atmosphere, and because these tools are simple and always available, we use them. Others see us using these tools so effectively that they adopt them. Seeking joy is contagious!

Teri is a great example of changing struggle into joy. She and I met for just one hour and she solved a problem that has been haunting her for a couple of years. Teri started our meeting saying, "I am drinking too much I know, and in the morning I tell myself I won't drink that night, then about 6:00 when I get home from work, I have a glass of wine. By the end of the night 2/3 of the bottle is gone. And the next morning I tell myself 'O.K., tonight I won't drink.' Morning after morning, night after night it is the same thing. My fiancé said he was worried about me. He said I smelled like alcohol every night. I was defensive and I assured him I only have one or two glasses a night, at the most. Then I asked myself "Why am I lying?"

"I went to AA at lunchtime, but by the end of the session I was exhausted. Those poor people, they have lost so much. If I keep drinking, I could be like them. I'm done with alcohol. I have to stop. That night I went home, worked in the garden, rode my bike and didn't drink. But the next night at 6:00 sharp I found myself with my glass of Bordeaux. Am I an alcoholic? I have gone to three meetings and I know I should look for similarities not differences, but nothing bad has happened from my drinking and I just don't think AA is going to work for me."

We talked about using the ABC's of **Bounce** to create a lifestyle that would make it easier for her to live the way she wants. Rather than blaming stress or busyness, Teri came up with a plan. First, she decided not to drink for a year. She didn't drink when she was pregnant or nursing, so this was far less daunting than never drinking again.

She decided to change her evening routine and have a snack on her way home before picking up her kids, so that she wasn't hungry or thirsty. She decided to bring a snack for the kids to have in the car, so that instead of making dinner as soon as they got home, they could ride bikes or go for a walk. If the weather was bad she could read them or watch TV together.

She decided to make double recipes of some of their favorite dinners—spaghetti, baked chicken, and bean soup—and put it in the freezer so when they came back she could heat the dinner and not spend so much time in the kitchen where she had regularly poured her first glass of wine. She decided she and the kids would start making dinner together and set the table so it was pretty. They could make decorations and learn some table etiquette. It would be fun.

Teri said thoughtfully, "Sometimes I am afraid I won't sleep so I have wine to help me relax. Now my plan is that when the kids go to bed, I will meditate for half an hour. Then I'll pick up around the house, read or watch TV until 10 and go to bed."

Two weeks later Teri reported, "I've always liked journaling, so I started writing about my successes of the day, including time playing with the kids, exercising, working in the garden, and reading. I started making green tea—having it when I sat down at night—and I started doing crossword puzzles. At noon, I started going for a walk or listening to my meditation CD. I had always made us a good breakfast, but sometimes I would skip lunch. Now I make sure I pack some veggies and I have a snack mid-morning, lunch, late afternoon snack, then dinner. I feel like I am back in charge of my life. I have plenty of energy and I always feel good. The kids are happier and more relaxed, too. I had my old 2/3 bottle of wine one night, and I thought 'Oh no. Here I go.' But I didn't. I got back on my plan and that was that."

It has now been three months since Teri had wine. She says, "Moving ahead, doing what I needed to do for myself first made all the difference. The other part that worked was that it was so easy. Now my sister is bouncing to lose weight. **Bounce** *works—go MENTAL!"*

MENTAL

Move *Experience* *Nourish*

Touch *Appreciate* *Laugh*

Just Go

I am not an athletic person, so exercise takes effort for me. As our **Bounce** group talked about the **Bounce Basics**, several of us groaned, "Yes, we should exercise, but . . . !" We all agreed that the single most important thing we should do to make ourselves healthier and happier immediately is exercise.

We discussed our own reluctance, we talked about how to make it easier for ourselves, and we came up with the idea of reminding ourselves to simply MOVE. Take the stairs instead of the elevator, carry our own groceries to the car, park away from the store entrance when shopping, we listed all the little things we can do to get incidental exercise.

Thinking about exercising does not create more endorphins, unfortunately, so I walk. And when I walk, I look for beauty and I set a timer, otherwise I distract myself by checking my watch. I can usually persuade myself to go for a speedy walk for half an hour, focused on the reflection of light in the mud puddle or the buds on the trees. I get increased endorphins just for being in the moment looking for beauty.

I have also found that if I set a routine, leave the house at 7:30 a.m., back by 8 a.m.—just go—I remind myself without an internal debate. Go! Here is where the thinking part comes in. I get an extra dose of endorphins for feeling proud of myself for taking my half-hour walk.

It doesn't matter if you walk, run, roller blade, do pilates or hike, just go –MOVE!

Move

MENTAL

You can tell if you are getting a full dose of endorphins because it becomes hard to breathe. When your muscles use up all their stored glucose and are using only oxygen, you get an endorphin surge. The best exercises for an endorphin hit are running, swimming, cross-country skiing, long-distance rowing, bicycling, or aerobics.

Aerobics, according to the American College of Sports Medicine, is "any activity that uses large muscle groups, can be maintained continuously, and is rhythmic in nature." And it makes both the heart and lungs work hard.

The important issue is to get moving, find something you like doing and pick up the pace, or do it a little longer, just push yourself a bit. It is good for you. Be sure that you tell yourself that you are proud of you. You can get two of your **Bounce** Essentials playing a sport that includes other people like baseball, basketball, or simply, tag. Running around while laughing with friends gives you a triple dose of endorphins. So play frisbee, catch, or just fool around while changing your mind and changing your life.

151

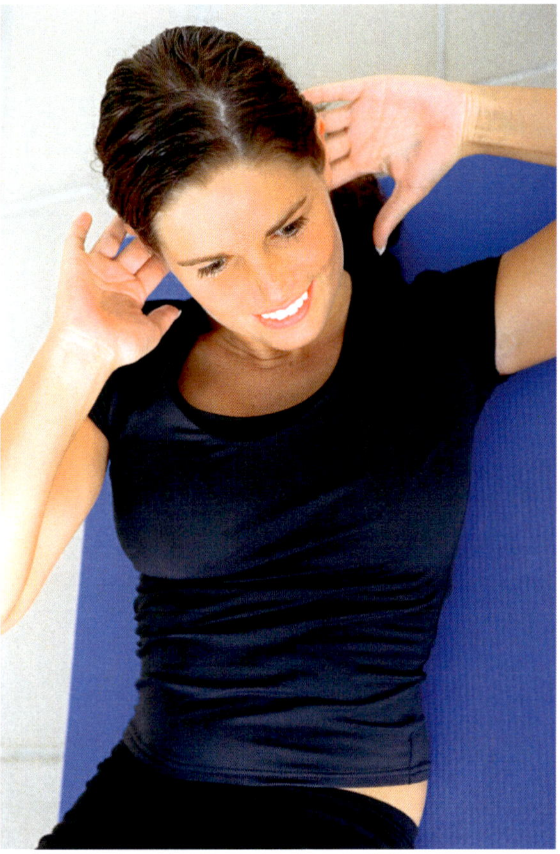

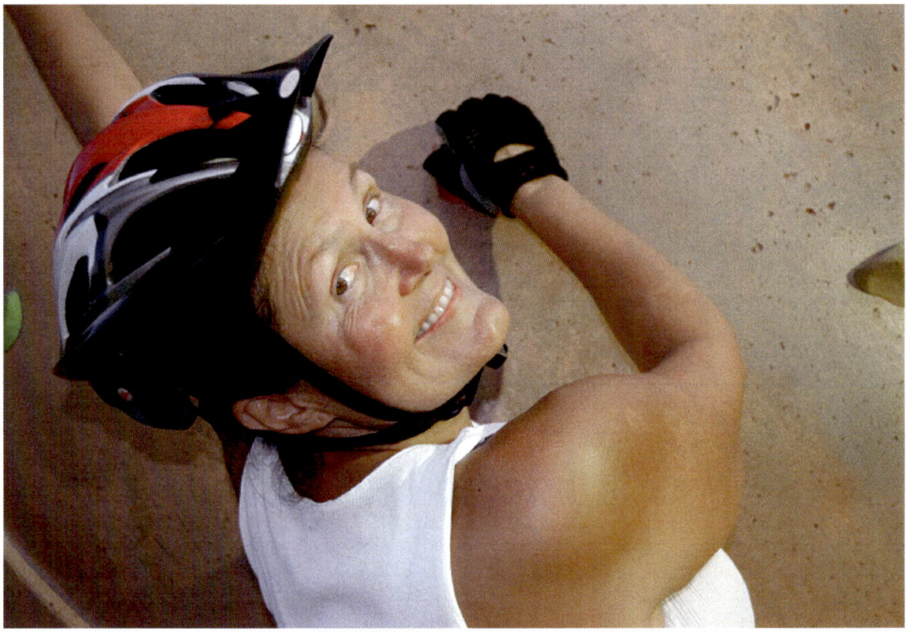

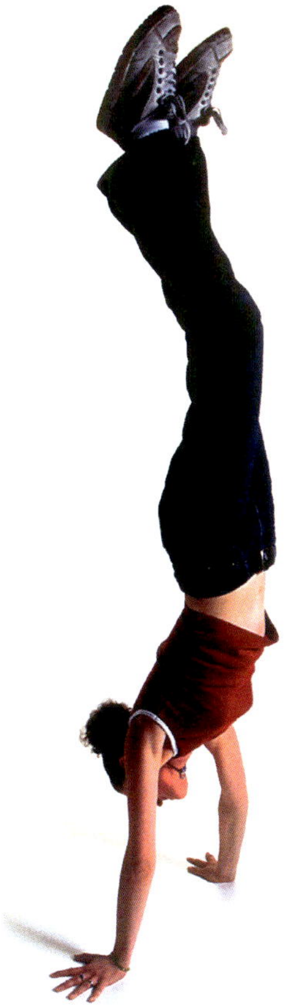

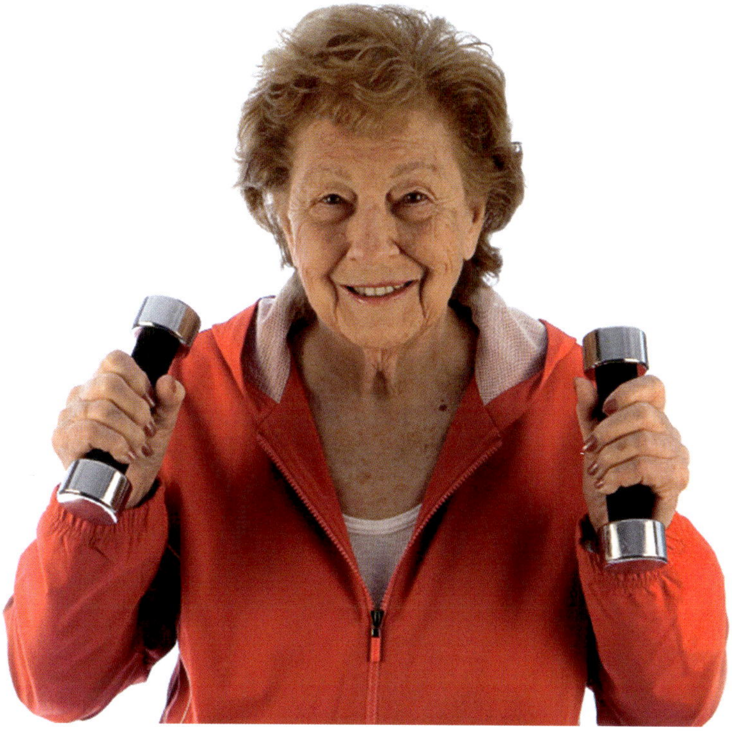

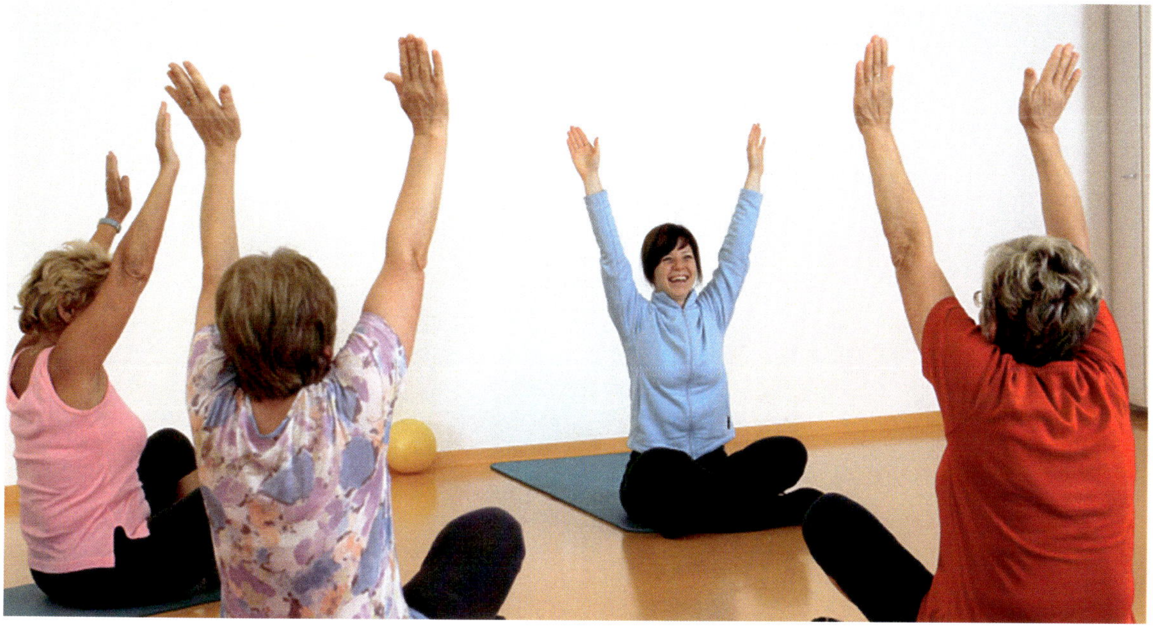

Be in the Moment

Experience means being fully present in the moment, aware of all that is within you and around you. Being fully available to yourself by quieting your mind, allowing yourself peace. Only then can you be sensually aware of your self and your environment. Because of the difficulty most of us have "quieting our minds," please, consider trying it. It is easy and makes a big difference.

Experience involves heightening your senses. Smell the fresh flowers, hear the birds singing, taste the delicate flavor of fresh bread, see the beauty of a rainbow, and touch the cheek of someone you love. Be a sensualist—it stimulates your brain and gives you a nice dose of endorphins. Enjoy the day-to-day beauty that your senses know, and be engaged in the moment.

Be in the moment, and fully experience your senses.

Experience

MENTAL

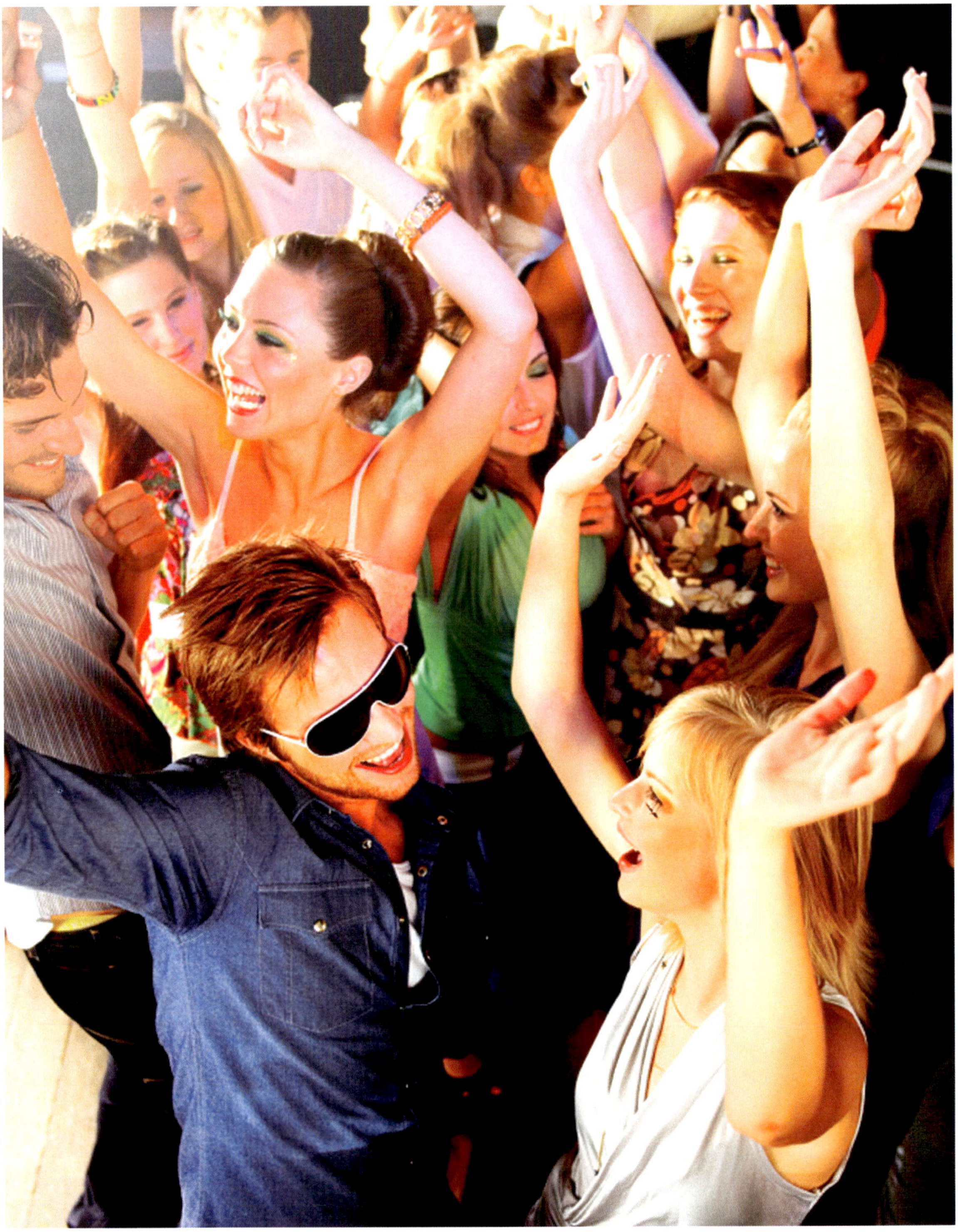

157

Feel joy!

Take a moment to snap a picture, whether you have a camera, or not.
Look for beauty and pause to enjoy.

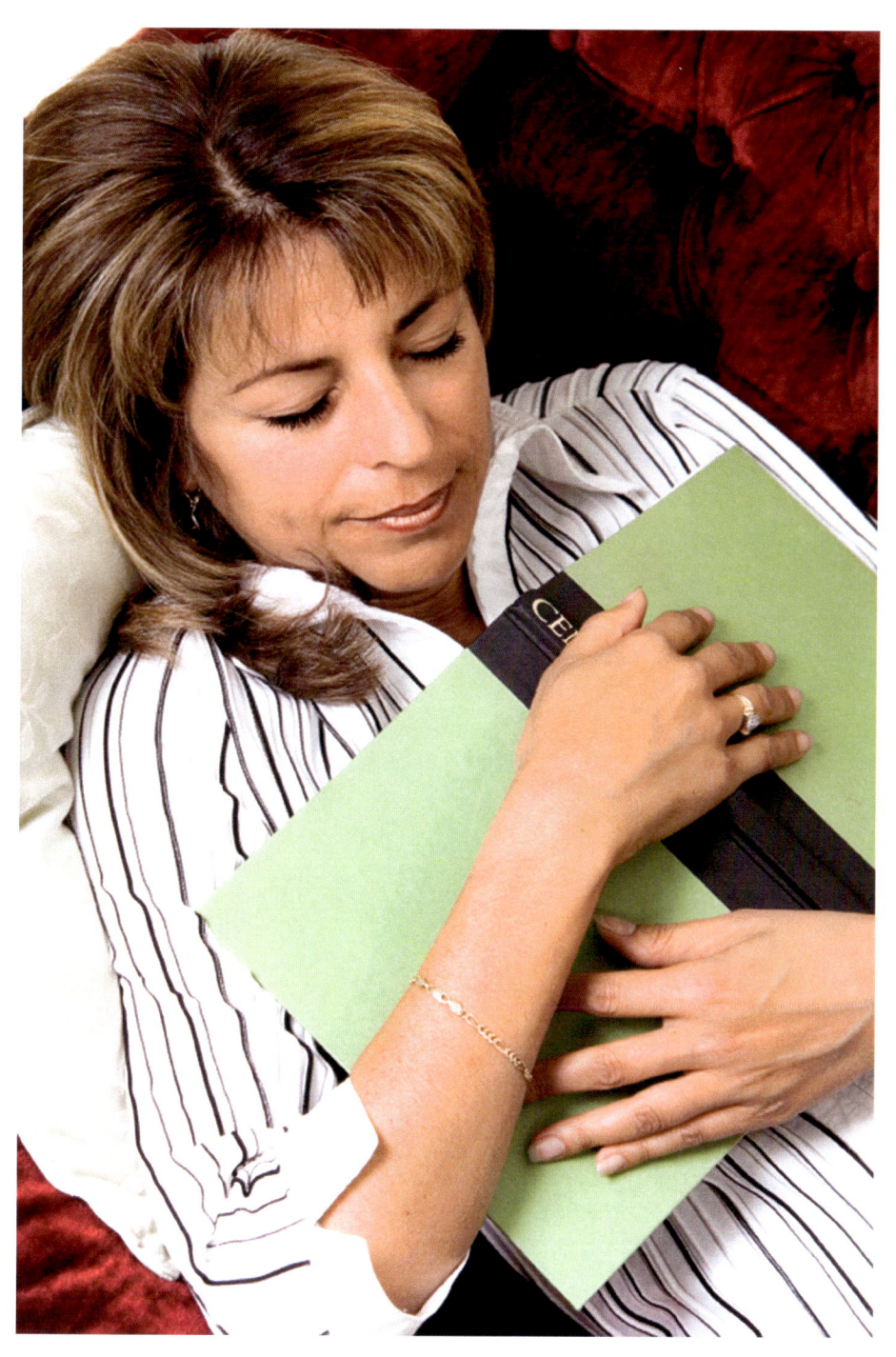

*The more that you read, the more things you will know.
The more you learn, the more places you'll go."
– Dr. Seuss, I Can Read with My Eyes Shut!*

Eat Simply

Healthy food is important to the nourishment of your body and your mind. Good nourishment provides a bounty of endorphins and is easy—if you keep it simple. This is an area where the busyness of our lives can interfere with our health—unnecessarily.

Creating rituals for yourself helps keep it simple. Eat at the same times daily. Create a pleasant environment for yourself when preparing food. A negative offshoot of fancy kitchenware is the complexity that comes with all the stuff. Eliminate the stuff and keep the kitchen clean and simple, with healthy, fresh foods.

Eat simple, fresh, local foods and nourish your mind and body.

The Mediterranean style of eating emphasizes foods rich in natural oils and is good for your heart.

Nourish

M E N T A L

Eat fresh. A simple rule is eat what you could grow. Shop for groceries that travel the minimal distance to get to you.

We think of avoiding fat when we chose healthy food but fat is necessary for the body to function and two of our most important fats are omega-3 fatty acids and omega-6s. The multiple benefits of omega-3s include: reducing the risk of heart disease and stroke; lowering blood pressure; relieving depression; limiting attention deficit disorder (ADD); eliminating joint pain and other rheumatoid problems; alleviating skin ailments. Some research suggests omega-3s can boost the immune system. Research indicates that omega-3s encourage the production of endorphins when helping to control inflammation in the joints, the bloodstream, and tissues.

Nuts, seeds and unrefined whole grains are filled with Omega-3s but are not a very great range of foods. So unless you are eating a lot of seeds and whole grains every day you are probably not getting enough omega-3s. Using bottled oils, such as soy, rape and walnut oils, on salads and in cooking isn't enough. Olive oil contains very low omega-3 and is low in omega-6.

Fatty fish, like salmon, mackerel, herring, sardines, or trout and nuts, seeds, and unrefined whole grains are primary sources of omega-3s. Foods such as whole-grain cereals (shredded wheat or oat flakes), starches like brown rice and raisins, pecans, walnuts or hazelnuts sprinkled on salads all help in getting enough omega-3s.

Omega-6s are found in foods such as eggs, poultry, cereals, vegetable oils, baked goods, and margarine. Omega-6s are also considered essential. Omega-6s, the so-called bad fats, are also necessary for the body to be healthy. They support skin health, lower cholesterol, and help make our blood "sticky" so it is able to clot.

When omega-3s and -6s are appropriately balanced, all is well, but excess omega-6s lead to major inflammatory problems throughout the body. Because fats burn quickly, we need a fresh supply daily, and omega-3s are not popular in America and are less readily available. Research suggests around 9g per day of omega-6 and 6g per day of omega-3 oils for general health (1.5 to 1 ratio of omega-6 to omega-3).

To get the full endorphin benefit, take a moment when the food first touches your tongue and let it rest there. Focus your brain only on the taste, just for two seconds. Seek joy in eating.

Epicatechin improves blood flow and thus seems good for cardiac health. Cocoa, the major ingredient of dark chocolate, is loaded with epicatechin and has been found to have nearly twice the antioxidant content of red wine and up to three times that of green tea.

The Journal of Human Nutrition and Dietetics reported guarana to be effective for weight loss, improved memory and increased physical endurance. It is also an effective antioxidant. Guarana is a plant extract that is added to energy drinks.

Grass-fed beef and lamb contain omega 3s.

Control the Radicals

Flavonoids have been referred to as "nature's biological response modifiers" because of evidence on their ability to modify the body's reaction to allergens, viruses, and carcinogens. They show anti-allergic, anti-inflammatory, anti-microbial and anti-cancer activity. In addition, flavonoids act as powerful antioxidants, protecting against oxidative and damage from free-radicals.

Flavonoids have a role in the prevention of cancers and cardiovascular disease. The beneficial effects of fruit, vegetables, and tea, or even red wine have been attributed to compounds rather than to known nutrients and vitamins.

Quercetin is a flavonoid that forms the "backbone" for many other flavonoids. Quercetin is an anti-inflammatory agent because it interferes with inflammation. For example, it restricts both the creation and the release of histamines known to create allergic reactions. Keeping fruit and vegetables available for snacks helps you get your flavonoids.

Apples, onions, raspberries, black and green teas, red wine, red grapes, citrus fruit, cherries, broccoli, and leafy green vegetables are the best sources of quercetin. Avoid supplements, eat the real thing.

Good sources of flavonoids include all citrus fruits, berries, onions, parsley, legumes, green tea, red wine, seabuckthorn, and dark chocolate (with a cocoa content of 70% or greater).

Green and black teas are good for the brain and have antioxidant benefits.

Reach Out

Touch is physically connecting with another. The sense of touch is transmitted through our skin, our largest sensory organ. There are many ways to touch, reach out, and extend making contact with another being, person, pet, or nature. The sense of belonging is met through touch as well as self-esteem needs. Touch is a primary biological need with sexual touch being important in staying young and healthy. Sex important for mind, body and marriage.

Lynn and I were traveling to a remote island in Canada when he started having an irregular heartbeat. We went to the emergency room, where he was promptly hooked up to the usual arsenal of machinery. I sat beside him while he dozed, holding his hand as we waited for test results. Then I started lightly massaging his arm. With each caress his blood pressure dropped. I tried massaging his head, same result. I stopped, up it went. I massaged, down it came. It was not a very scientific experiment, but it was impressive to me.

There have been countless studies on the benefit of touching dogs or cats for the elderly, but touch awakens the senses and releases endorphins. Reach out and touch someone.

Touch

MENTAL

170

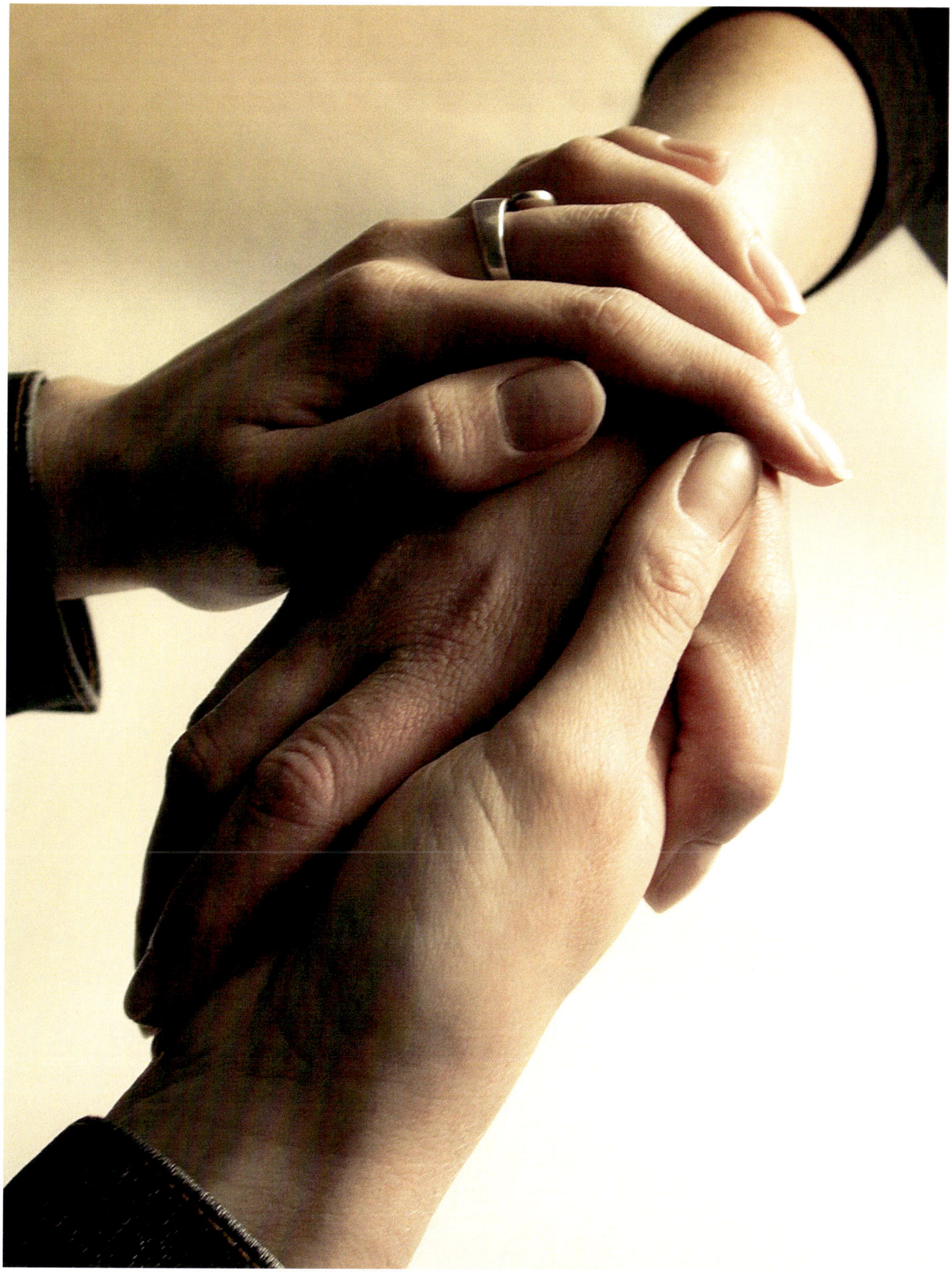

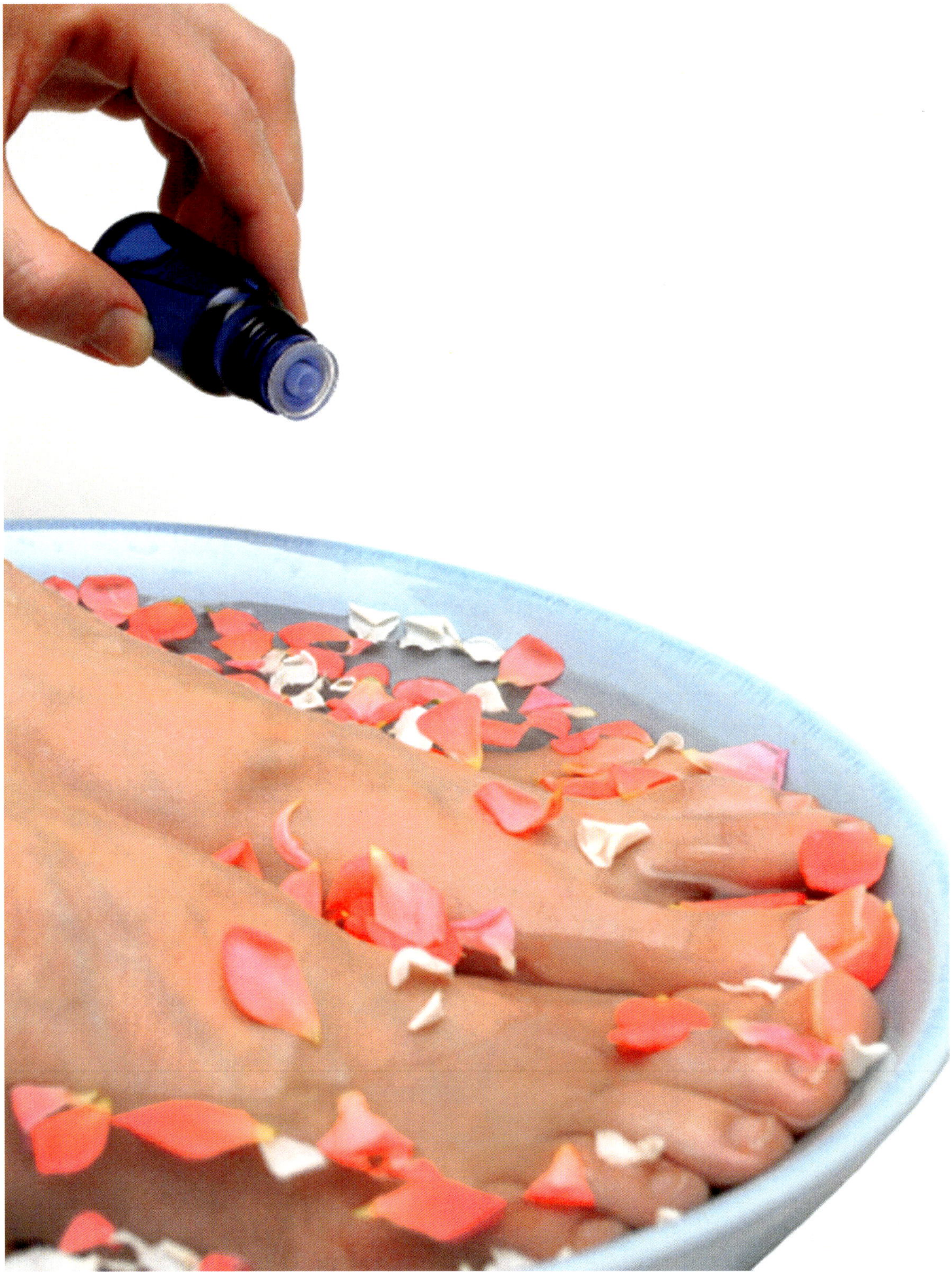

173

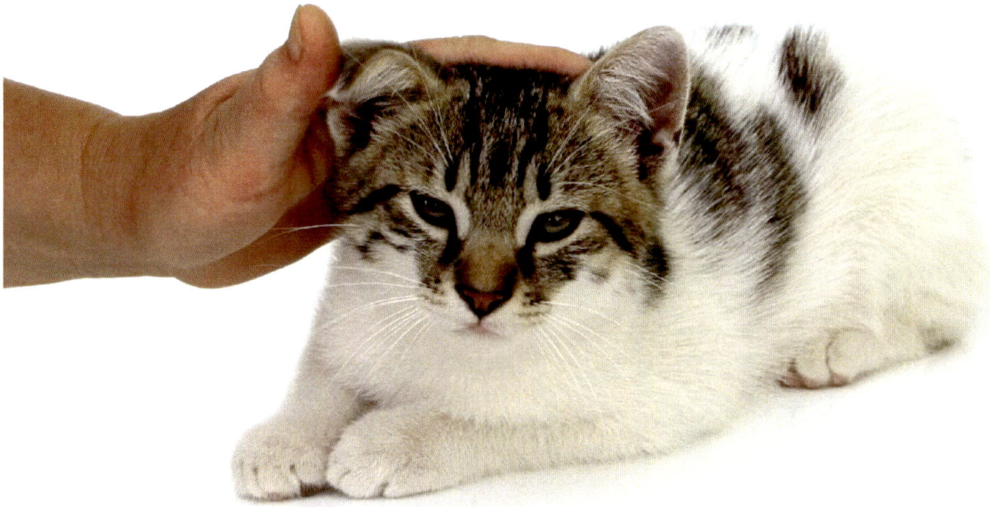

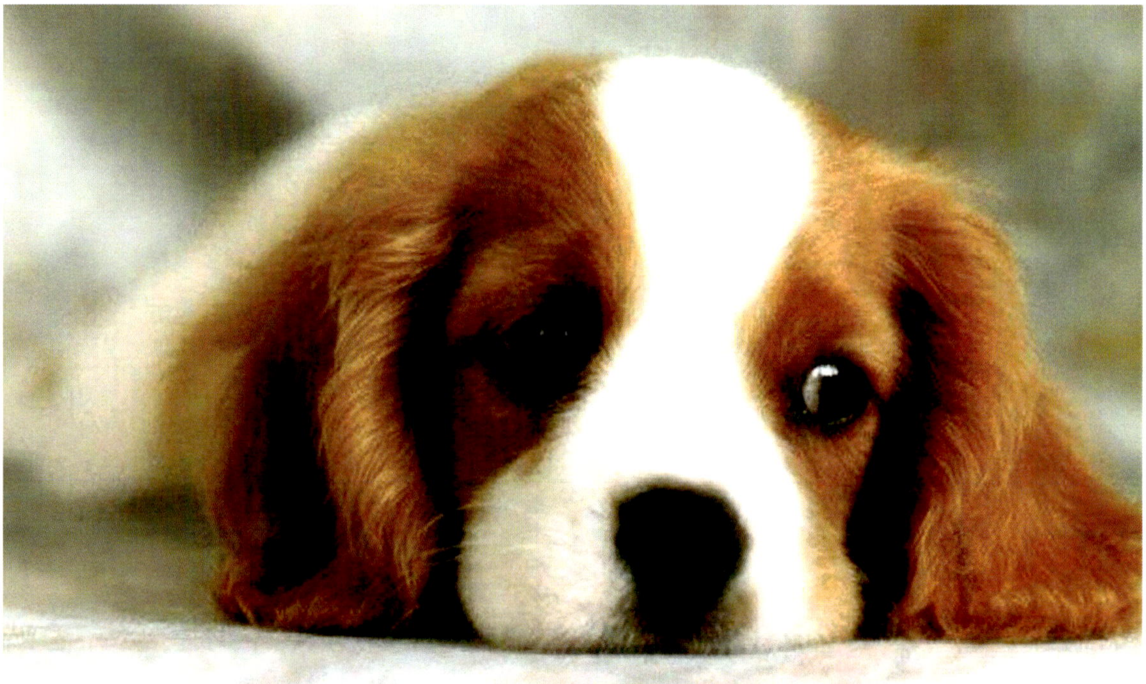

175

Spread Joy

Great delight and happiness are packed with endorphins, and the more you spread them around the more *you* get. That's right, when you give someone else a bundle of joy in the form of gratitude or appreciation they get a hit of endorphins and so do you. And it is contagious. One smile, one compliment, or one thank you leads to many others.

Self-esteem needs are met by recognition, appreciation and respect, so when we step forward in a relationship to meet the needs of others, *we* get rewarded with the miraculous benefit of endorphins, too.

Spreading joy through appreciation is something we should think of as a one-a-day vitamin. In fact, endorphins are probably just as important. I went to pick up office supplies and was having trouble finding the right ink cartridge for my printer. A young man went to the back room and couldn't find the cartridge I needed. I thanked him and left. I stopped for coffee and bought an extra cup and a little chocolate bar and took it back to him. When I gave it to him, he gasped, "Why?" "Just spreading joy," I said. He laughed, "O.K.! I'll pass it on!"

Spread joy by taking a few minutes to show your appreciation!

Appreciate

MENTAL

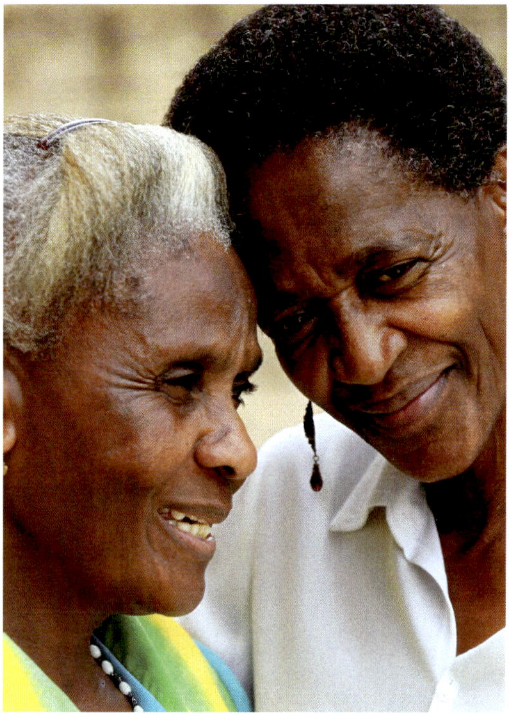

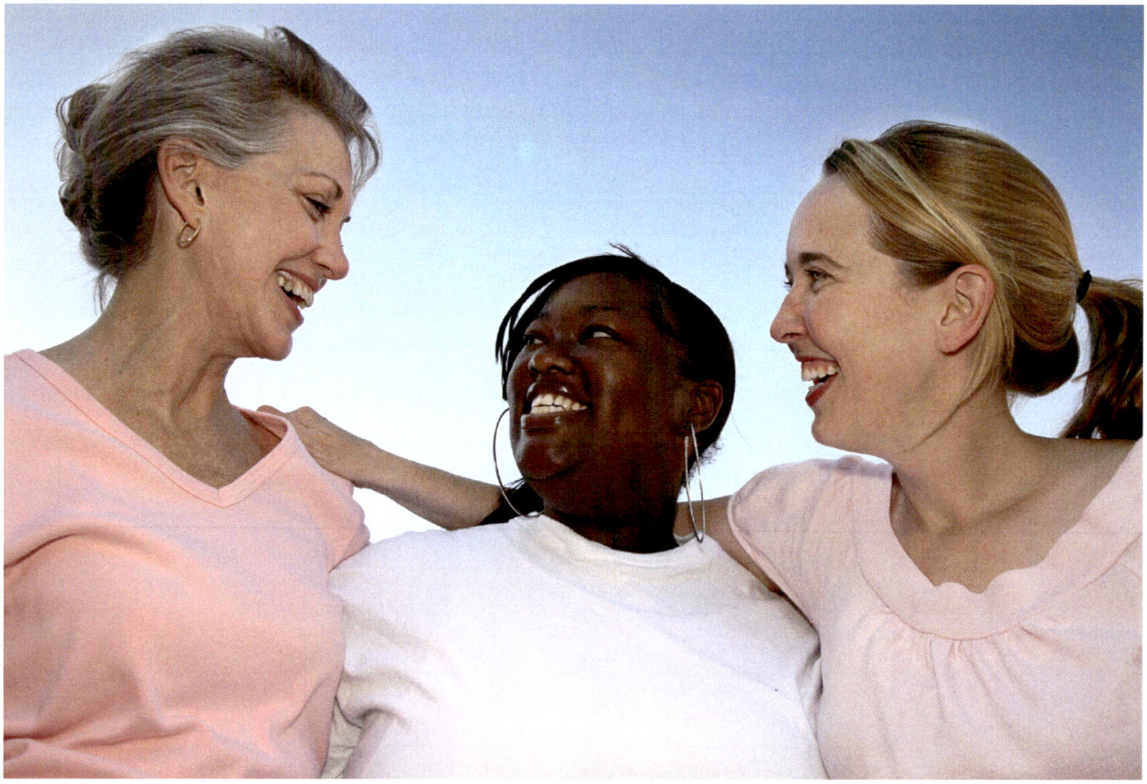

179

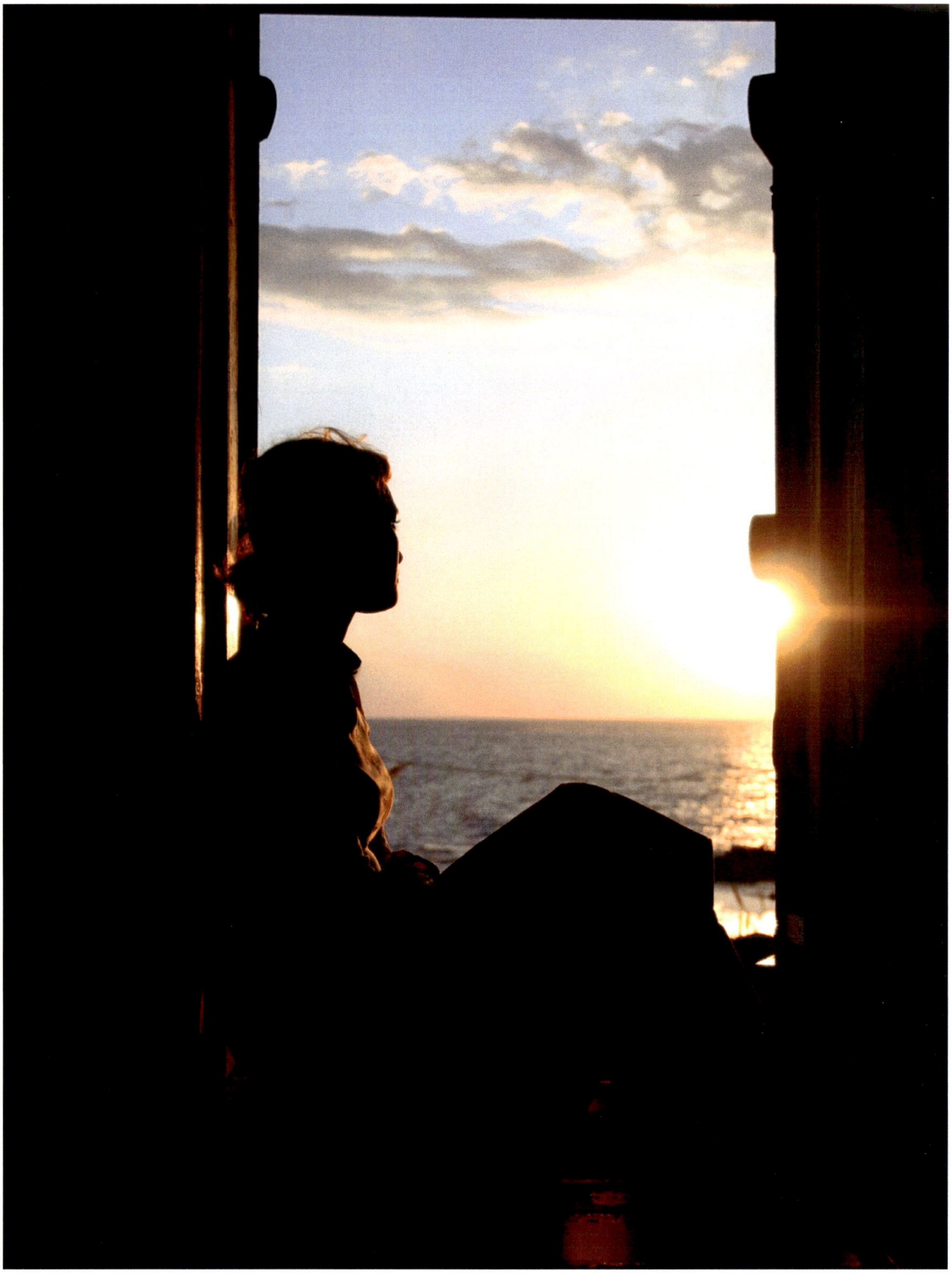

Be thoughtful and appreciative, spread joy!

Live, Love

Laughter *is* the best medicine, it turns out. Laughter reduces steroid hormones like cortisol and increases the number of endorphins and antibodies. Beyond the benefits to the brain the body gets a little workout. The diaphragm contracts the abs and the muscles in the shoulder get a bit of exercise, leaving muscles relaxed. Laughter gives us the nudge to see things a bit lighter and shift the mind from serious or threatening to something light-hearted and less earth shattering. Nearly everything has a funny side when you really think about it.

And laughter is contagious, so not only do you get endorphins, so do those around you. If you don't laugh easily, practice. Fake it till you make it, a study where participants were asked to put a pencil in their mouth, mimicking a smile, produced the same endorphin release as the real thing. Laughter is a cleanser—sweeping away emotional stress—and an endorphin bonanza. Live, love, laugh, it's good for you and everyone around you!

Laugh

Look for laughs. Buy a joke book or search the joke-loaded Internet. Watch late night TV and have a pencil and paper ready because you will probably want to write them down so you can remember. Half the endorphin benefit is in retelling.

Get friends and go to the comedy club, not as a critic, but as an excuse to laugh. Plan a game night playing something where everyone has an equal chance to win, like charades, bingo, liars dice or Yahtzee. Be silly!

MENTAL

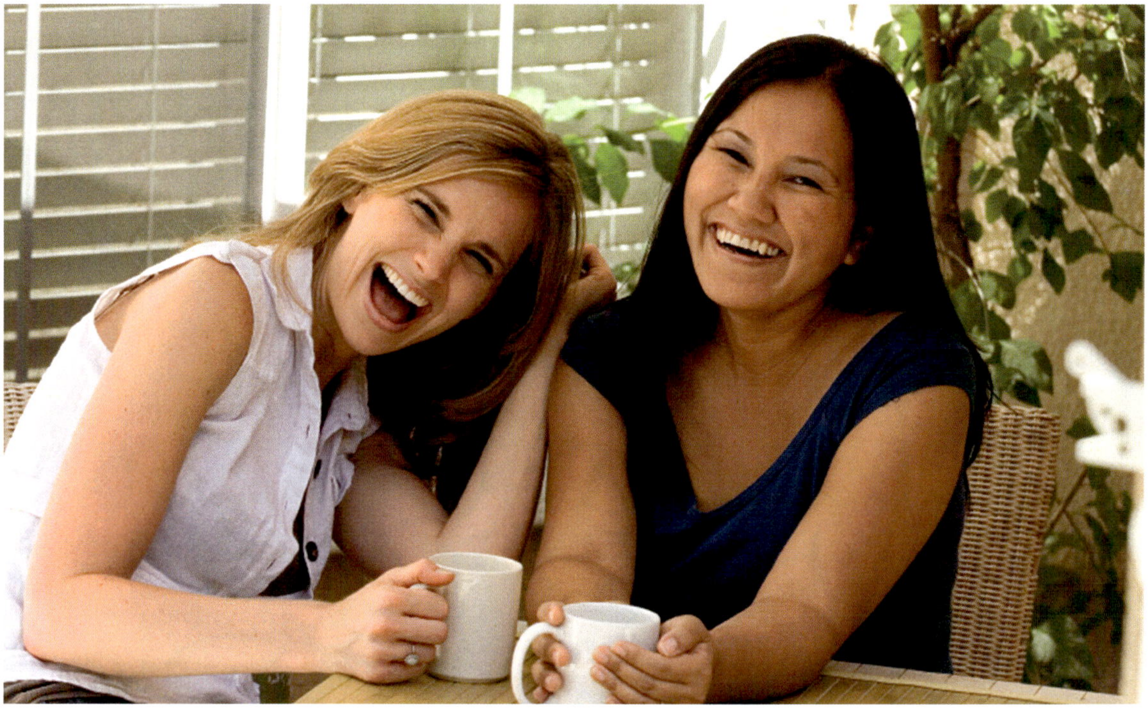

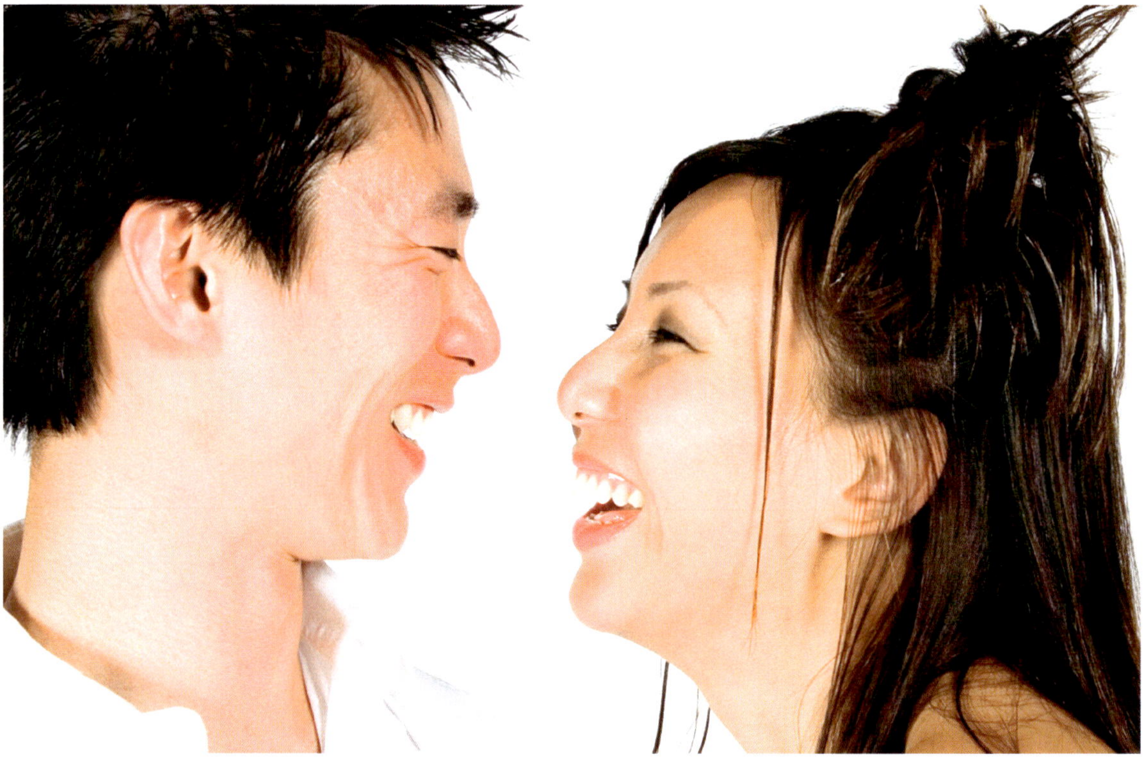

185

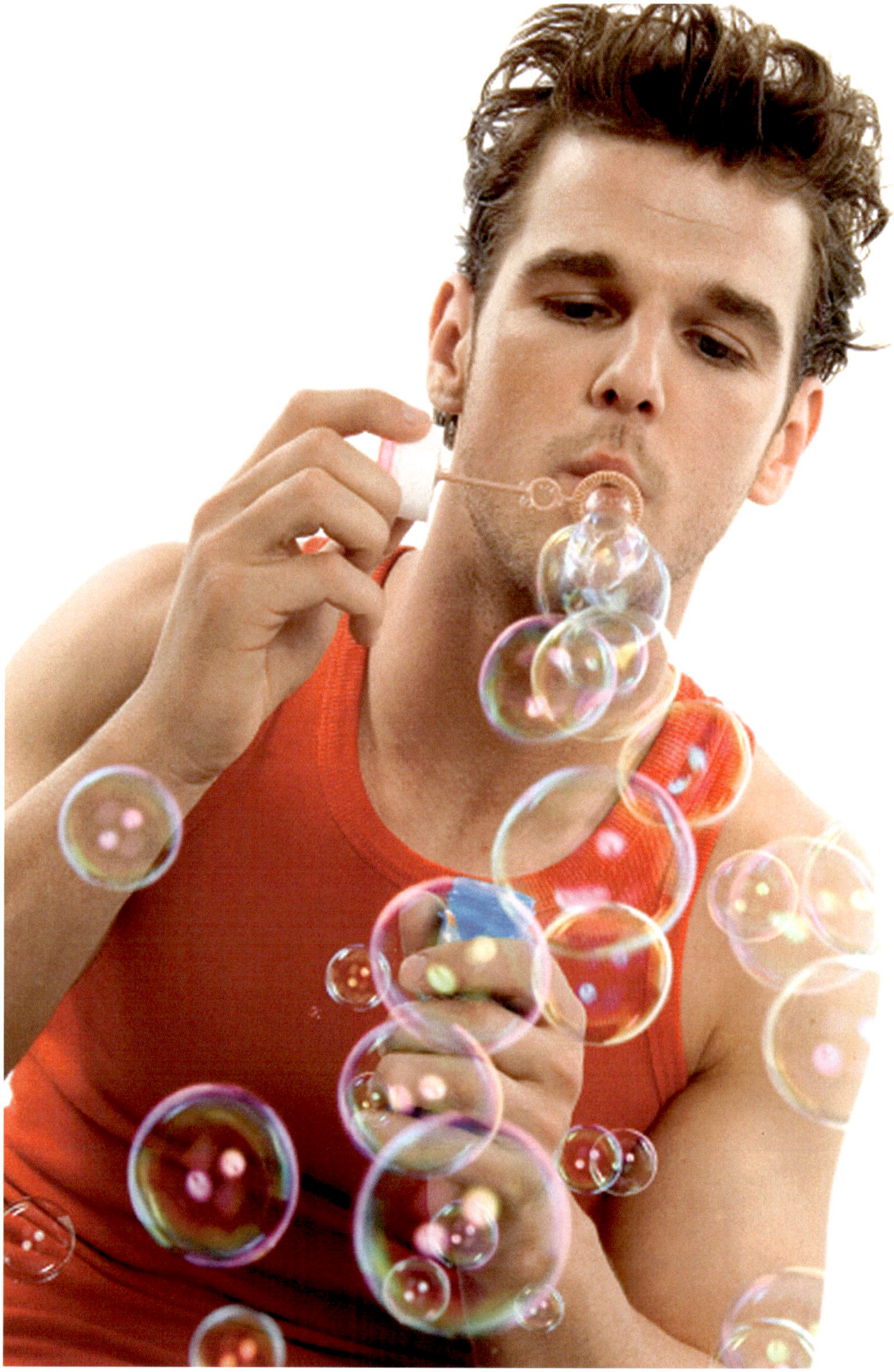

187

Bounce Transformations

Bounce, Be Transformed is a way of life for us—the original ***Bounce*** women. I have told you some of our stories and stories of friends and clients with the hope that they will inspire you to bounce into the next phase of your own life. The risk of change is less than the risk of staying the same. ***Bounce*** women choose growth and transformation. We are intentional in pursuing lives of personal transformation, seeking both joy and meaning in daily life.

I am going to end with two more stories, Susan's then Sarah's transformations. First, Susan. Susan lived a sheltered childhood filled with love, opportunity and joy, but adult life dealt her some hard blows in the world of love and loss. Giving up on love would have been understandable—divorce, death and desertion all left her wounded and uncertain, but she decided to bounce into love and—love **completely.**

As the only child of an air traffic controller and a homemaker, I felt loved and cherished by my parents. My mother, determined not to have a spoiled, only child, but a well-rounded one, filled my days with dance lessons, both ballet and tap. I took swimming, tennis, ice-skating and horse-back riding lessons as well. I had a very happy, fun-filled childhood and teen years.

After graduation from high school, I wanted to go to New York City to dance, but my parents said, "NO." Their wishes prevailed and I was college-bound. Two years into college I was restless. I wanted to get away from home and do something by myself for the summer. I saw an ad to be a Playboy bunny and I was going. My parents had made all my decisions for me up to this point, but this time was different. I wanted to decide for myself and I clearly remember my father saying to my mother, "Beth, she's going. This is the first time Susan hasn't asked our permission to do something." I went. I spent three months at the Baltimore Playboy hutch, and a very protective staff sent me back to college in the fall—virginity intact.

At 22, I married a handsome young doctor. He was my dream come true, and I loved him. My mother and I had dreamed of my beautiful wedding, but that was not something my husband believed in, so it did not happen. His dismissal of my dream should have been a warning of what life with him would be like, but I was too naive. Living with him was like living with my parents; he made all the decisions. We went to counseling and I wanted to make it work, but by age 30 I knew I had to have a voice in my own life. Our marriage ended after 12 years. My heart ached.

I had always been athletic so it seemed natural that I became a fitness trainer. I got a job on cruise ship line, traveled the world, scuba dived, and had a wonderful time. The time away helped me heal. This was the growing-up time I had missed in my 20s. Time that I needed to be a fully alive adult.

I was 38 when I married my second husband; he had two children. I wanted a family and his kids became a major focus of our lives and I liked being with them. He said that I helped them heal from the wounds of his divorce and the first years of our marriage were good. Sometimes the kids were hard for me to understand. I wasn't their mother; I was their dad's wife. But at other times we were close and they confided in me and we loved each other. I certainly gave them my best effort.

After about 10 years of marriage, he and I were not getting along very well. I was concerned about his health. He had gained weight and was sitting around watching too much TV, plus his blood pressure was high. He would clam up when I brought it up. When I said he didn't seem like himself and was irritable, he flew into a rage.

We were married for 11 years when we went scuba diving for the last time. The dive had been entirely normal, good weather and no complications. But when he surfaced, he waved for help. I knew something was wrong. When we first got him aboard, he seemed alright, but within half an hour it became evident that he was having difficulty breathing. We made it to the hospital where a very experienced and caring staff treated him. He was getting better and I was making arrangements to bring him back to the U.S. when the doctor called me to come to the hospital immediately. He died shortly after I arrived. Much of the rest of that year was a blur. I felt like I was living a dream, a bad dream. But, I thought, I still had my family. I was wrong.

I have since learned from other step-parents, my family died with him. I wanted to be emotionally and financially present for his children. I cared for them the best I knew how as their stepmother, and I gave them substantial amounts of money from their Dad's and my estate after his death. Still within a couple of years, they were gone, and, sadly, I have no contact with them now.

I thought to myself that I'd had enough tries at love, and I had lost every time. Enough of this pain. But with coaxing and coaching from friends, I made an effort at Internet dating, without much enthusiasm, until I connected with one man who lived 2,000 miles away. Great—a long distance relationship. I didn't need that, but still we kept talking. Having had two failed loves and struggle with the loss of my family, I was very reluctant to love again.

After a year, he said he could move to Seattle. I wanted him to be close, but I was afraid. I agreed to our living together, but no marriage I told myself. But a year after he moved to Seattle, I had made the decision to love completely, no holding back and no tiptoeing around it. I don't know that there was a day I changed my mind, but I was conscious of making a very intentional decision to go ahead and love him—100%. I knew if I was going to love again, it would have to be completely. So, I jumped in.

We have been together seven years now. I am very happily married and I know the reason. I treat my husband like the man of my dreams, which he is. Knowing that love can fade or be lost, I have been determined to keep our passion alive. Of course, in the beginning it was effortless, but as we became less engaged with each other I saw the danger, so I started a wonderful tradition: Saturday afternoon play dates.

Just like anything else in our busy lives, we schedule play dates, intimate sexual fun time, into the calendar. Play dates are how we stay connected. It is more than time for sex. It is time to be silly or serious, frivolous or intense, seductive or sensual. I think our play dates add energy and excitement to our marriage, and we both enthusiastically look forward to Saturdays.

Sometimes we play risqué games like strip poker or we may watch a sweet romantic movie. I am usually the one who plans it. I like to play dress-up and seduce him, and I like it when he surprises me with a tiny teddy. We can feed each other yummy goodies or share a glass of champagne. Whatever we do, we laugh a lot and are totally focused on each other.

I am so glad I took the chance and bounced into loving again, all the way. I love **Bounce**.

There is more to Susan's story than her very loving and passionate marriage. Susan transformed herself in other ways. Seeking joy and pleasure, she decided to get her body back in shape.

At one of our many **Bounce** meetings focused on how to communicate what we were learning, the **Bounce** women were talking about what we needed to do daily to be our best. We talked a lot about exercise, and how we could get ourselves moving. Susan took it further. Move made her think about her own love of dance and other kinds of movement. She already took dance lessons and entered several dance competitions. She and her husband enjoyed dancing.

One thing led to another and she decided to get serious. She was about 25+ pounds over her best weight and she wanted to get fit—and strong. In her early 30s, long before it was popular, Susan became a body-builder without drugs. She decided to do it again, and be a 58-year-old body-builder, again with no steroid drugs.

She took money she had set aside for a special birthday party and invested in a body-building trainer. Her workouts were daily, five days a week. She has gained strength and stamina over the past year and entered a national body-building competition in October. She came in second in the division for women over 35 years old. Those extra pounds are long gone and Susan's energy is vibrant; she is effusively happy. What a bounce!

And, as usually happens with **Bounce**, her transformation has taken her down another new path. She has decided to explore combining her passion for exercise and her sensuality and is teaching women's health with a focus on sensuality. Susan's life is full of love, joy and meaning. She is living at her 90%+ level, bouncing happily along.

The next Bounce story is Sarah's. She has written this story, so it is in her own words.

191

Sarah suffered during her divorce, now she has fallen in love with a man who is recently divorced and still recovering. He has two young adult daughters. Anyone who goes through a divorce knows that it is emotionally difficult to remember the good in your former spouse because of all the wounds. It is all too common for battling former spouses to become enemies. New partners of the recently divorced asily view the former spouse as the villan, feeling more empathy for their lover than his former. Sarah moved herself beyond taking sides.

We walk together hand in hand towards the chairs placed in rows along the damp, grassy lawn. At 10:45 a.m. I am already warm from the early August morning sun and from my anticipation and uncertainty about how this day will turn out. The dozen cream-colored roses I carry in my arms look droopy, showing signs of wilting, but we made sure to have them nonetheless. The roses were part of our plan: to celebrate and acknowledge important passages. I am attending a graduation ceremony with Ron, the new man in my life. His daughter, Amelia, just completed the nursing program at Seattle University where we mingle among other families waiting for the nursing students to receive their special "pinning."

I wear a short, white skirt with gold horizontal stripes, a white camisole top and a gold silk long-sleeved sweater. My earrings and chunky gold bracelet match my gold and black braided sandals. I chose this outfit intentionally. On previous occasions, friends and family have said, "Wow, that color sweater looks great on you." I am deliberate about choosing what makes me feel and look my best.

We select seats midway to the stage. Everyone has umbrellas up to guard against the intense sun. I keep my umbrella closed, because I want a clear view. I look over at Ron. He has sweat on his face. He is intent. Ron is recently divorced. I know his ex-wife will be at the ceremony, so I am feeling a little intimidated, not sure what to expect. Ron and I have talked about this situation ahead of time. So I have come prepared with a plan. My plan includes the words I want to say to her, and the tone with which I want to say them. I have discovered I gain more confidence with the power of a plan.

*I have empathy for Ron. I was married for 27 years. My husband left without warning, married a women he worked with, then announced he had a one-year-old son. I have empathy for my ex-husband, also. I have always wanted to come full circle with him after the divorce, to let him know that I accept his circumstances with compassion, and to embrace his new wife and child. But I have never felt I have had the opportunity. I feel now as though I might have the opportunity here, with Ron's ex-wife and boyfriend. To be my best self. To show acceptance, warmth, and kindness, and transcend all the negative feelings that seem to come with divorce. I am as happy as I have ever been in my life. My personal growth has taken some transformation, but **I know there is joy** in life after divorce.*

The ceremony starts. Speeches run about an hour. Then the master of ceremonies announces that each student will be presented with their pin, a ribbon placed around their neck, by a family member, friend, or significant person in their life. I turn to Ron and whisper, "Did Amelia mention this to you?" He shakes his head no. I imagine Amelia' mom will have the honor, and I am anxious to see her.

A long, hot, half an hour later, after watching student after student walk up to the podium, Amelia's name is finally called. I sit in my chair, sweating, determined to have full view of the stage, and to keep my carefully chosen outfit intact. Amelia is being "pinned" by her older sister, Helen. I feel joy in my heart for Ron. I touch his hand and squeeze the flesh firmly. He squeezes back. But I am genuinely disappointed, I have not yet seen or talked with Pauline. I turn to Ron and whisper, "Have you seen your ex yet?"

"No," he says. Maybe she's in the back."

My heart beats hard. At that moment, I realize my opportunity to meet her might disappear. I realize, also, how important this next step is for my personal growth. I know I need to take charge, to assert what I want, to meet Ron's ex-wife and her boyfriend, if I am ever going to come to terms with, and transcend my negative feelings about my own divorce.

I say to Ron, "I want to meet her."

"You sure?"

"Yes."

"Okay," he says.

We get up from our seats and quietly make our way back through the rows of chairs. I see Ron look around, hesitate, then start walking through the thick grass heading toward the far corner of the expansive green field toward two people, a man and a woman, sitting on a rock ledge. It takes us some time to reach them. I can see they are both staring at us, and I notice the woman stiffening. My heart beats fast. The man gets up as soon as we are directly in front of him.

Standing upright, Ron reaches out his hand and says, "Hi. I would like you to meet, Sarah." Pauline stands up, and I shake her hand and say. "It is a pleasure to meet you." Then I shake her boyfriend's hand, as does Ron. The man tells us that they found the coolest place in the field. I acknowledge with a smile, that yes, they were lucky, that I was sweating in my seat. Then I turn to Pauline, and say, "You have wonderful daughters. You have done a wonderful job raising them."

After a slight pause, she says, "Yes, they are great girls."

I say to both her and her boyfriend, "You are especially lucky they both have jobs in these times."

Ron turns towards them and says, "Well, maybe I'll see you around."

Ron and I turn and walk back across the grass until we get to the chairs. I stand quietly in the back next to Ron. I smile to myself, reveling in my feelings, until the ceremony ends fifteen minutes later. I had been my best self.

Wow! Wow! Wow! Wow comes to mind every time I think about my personal growth. My personal transformation. There simply is no other word for who I am now, versus who I was before **Bounce**. *With* **Bounce**, *I have been reborn. Not a trace of "the old Sarah" I tell myself! I am calm, cool, and collected. These are the words I use to describe myself, now. Before I was intense, hypersensitive, and acted impulsively with heightened emotions of anger, sadness, disgust, and oh, so much fear. Now, with* **Bounce**, *I live with joy and inner peace. My mantra is "living with love, joy, hope, makes a happy, healthy, whole, me." The Wow! comes from this realization: I can never go back to "the old Sarah." My brain no longer goes down automatic pathways. Instead it moves along new paths, recreated by my intentionality. That intentionality comes from* **Bounce**.

By practicing the **Bounce** *elements daily, I have transformed my life. Those essentials include my exercise. Eating foods that are nutritional and that I love. I plan out what I want to wear every day so that I choose those clothes that make me look and feel my best. When I feel at my worst, I cannot believe how many times I have completely turned my day around by simply styling my hair, putting on makeup, and wearing something I love! Now I seek out joy, first, above all else each day. I look at what my day holds, and I ask myself, what is the path that I find most joyful, and I move towards that path of least resistance. And I have learned to be grateful, appreciative, and compassionate.*

Through the process of transformation, now I often say, "Never in my wildest dreams did I imagine I would . . .

be a published author . . .

be able to "play" at my work . . .

be so effective in everything I touch . . .

be 100% responsible for my own emotional well-being and empowered enough to fulfill it . . .

find meaning and purpose in my life through the pure act of "joy" . . .

have enough control over my finances to feel secure . . .

fall in love without losing myself . . .

be with a man who fits into my life as easily as I fit into his . . .

Now, I truly am living my dream.

I chose Sarah's story for the final **Bounce** chapter because she tells not only how our own transformation continues but how it changes the lives of others. When we are intentional about how we live our lives, we hold ourselves to a higher standard. Holding ourselves to being our best means treating others in ways that allow them to be *their* best.

Sarah before **Bounce**

Sarah one year later, living **Bounce**

Bounce is a way of living that gives us the foundation to create a life based on joy and meaning. It requires only thought and intention—qualities we already possess. We all have *Bounce*; we use it after everyday hassles and inconveniences, and we can bounce and rebound after devastating events. During these difficult economic times the best investment you can make is in yourself, add Bounce to *your* life and the lives of those whose lives you touch.

Each time we treat others with respect and appreciation, they become better able to be their best. We all become what we are expected to be, and when the best is expected—we deliver. We ***Bounce! Bounce is contagious. When we spread joy, we change our minds and our lives.*** Sarah's story appears to be about a brief encounter on a summer day. She is not changing the world by brokering world peace. She is intentionally going out of her way to make someone else feel respected and acknowledged and maybe that helps create peace in their lives.

Sarah is not changing the world by feeding the world's starving children. She is simply showing Ron's daughters that she appreciates who they are and their mother's and father's success in rearing them. She is feeding the souls of four hungry people with a dose of endorphins. Sarah is simply living a life of joy and meaning, being intentional and thoughtful.

The Bounce women have learned that we must care for ourselves day to day in order to be fully capable of giving our best to a world that needs us. We go **MENTAL**, we **Move** by making sure we are out and about every day. We **Experience** by being present in the moment and by creating monthly outings that are new for us. **Nourish** comes in how and what we eat daily, finding pleasure in the simple elegance of fresh food. **Touch** ranges from hugs to handshakes or sometimes just a pat on the back. **Appreciate** is easy with lives so filled with the generosity of friends and strangers, we need to only take a few minutes a day to think about the kindness around us and within us. And, **Laugh**, we have gotten very good at laughing. We are deliberate is sharing cute jokes and finding humor in misunderstandings and new experiences. And, just for a little extra endorphin pleasure, we eat Seattle Chocolates!

I think Sarah's, Elizabeth's, Angela's, Katherine's, Susan's, Pepper's, Patricia's, and my own desire to live life being our best is what changes the world. Perhaps this *is* how we will feed the world's children, care for the planet and find world peace—each of us being our best—living lives of growth and transformation, seeking joy and meaning. The world needs all of us now—***Change your mind, change your life, change the world. Bounce, be transformed!***

Advisor and endorphin producer—Noir Staheli 4 year old Havanese

Appreciation

It is with sincere joy that I thank the women of *Bounce* for their generous participation in creating the book, the Circles and the movement. Their energy, time and willingness to experiment made the contributions of the *Bounce* women invaluable. My deepest gratitude to Susan Elliott, Sarah Williamson, Elizabeth Campbell, Partricia Verbryke, Pepper Schwartz, and Angela Turk. The actual creation of this book occurred because of the talents and gifts of Judy Dreis, Rosemary Woods and Angela Turk. I thank Jennifer Smith and Bradie Kvinsland, members of the *Bounce* group the first year, who left to work on *One Day at a Time* and *Life's Toughest Moments*. And, we miss Debbie Sawin. I am delighted to have Christy Alexander's help in reading, correcting and commenting on this book. And, Oh those chocolates from Jean Thompson and Seattle Chocolates, thank you.

I want all the women who have participated in the *Bounce* Circles to know I sincerely appreciate your willingness to change and share your wisdom with all of us. My thanks to Laurie Jonsson for encouragment and allowing me to speak about *Bounce* in China and Deb Healy for her organizing help.

This project ultimately touched just about everyone in my life. Their interest, advice, wisdom, perspective and sometimes tolerance enhanced the entire experience for me. First, my husband, Lynn T. Staheli, who contributed love and encouragement in addition to technical know-how. I appreciate the interest shown by my mother, Mildred Ribble, and my brother, Bruce, and son, Dalton. And I am especially grateful to my dear friend and sister-in-law, Kim Ribble, for her enthusiasm and wisdom. I thank our extended family Diane and Peter Demopulos, Linda Staheli and David Abramowitz, and Jeannette and Todd Staheli.

I value the zealous support of our friends in Turkey, Nadire Becker and Selim Yalcin. I thank my uncle, Dale Sponseller; and my aunts, Thelma Lake and Donna Sponseller; my cousin, Marcia Johnson; and second cousins, Jody Waite and Jennifer Copeland, for their unwavering personal support. In addition to the eight *Bounce* women who have become close friends, I am fortunate to have a larger circle of good friends whom I enjoy on a regular basis, Pat and Sheldon Pritchard, Francia Russell and Kent Stowell, Diane Adachi, Jeff McCord, Alan Honick, Sherry Raisbeck, Lars Jonsson, Betti Ann and Bob Yancey, Annette Polan, Cindy and Henry Burgess, Katie Clack, Denise Hopkins, Emily Wilson, Jayne Manlowe, Kim Martin, Sharon Lee, Nancy Zylstra, Pam Parker, Margaret Lahde and John Hennis, Travis Burgeson, Toni Whitney, Doreen Ellis, Betty Blount, Donna Waldhausen, Julie Jarmiolowski, Marla Beck, Jeannine Early, Debbie Lee, Patricia Comfort, Leslie Wolff, Gayle Duncan, and Lisa Lee.

Ingrid Pape-Sheldon shot the amazing photograph of me for the book, plus we had a lot of fun. And, I cannot forget the one who keeps me MENTAL every day, our dog, Noir.

A WOMAN SHOULD HAVE
by Pamela Redmond Satran

A WOMAN SHOULD HAVE . . .
Enough money within her control to move out and rent a place of her own even if she never wants to or needs to . . .

A WOMAN SHOULD HAVE . . .
Something perfect to wear if the employer or date of her dreams wants to see her in an hour . . .

A WOMAN SHOULD HAVE . . .
A youth she's content to leave behind . . .

A WOMAN SHOULD HAVE . . .
A past juicy enough that she's looking forward to retelling in her old age . . .

A WOMAN SHOULD HAVE . . .
A set of screwdrivers, a cordless drill, and a black lace bra . . .

A WOMAN SHOULD HAVE . . .
One friend who always makes her laugh . . . And one who lets her cry . . .

A WOMAN SHOULD HAVE . . .
A good piece of furniture not previously owned by anyone else in her family . . .

A WOMAN SHOULD HAVE . . .
Eight matching plates, wine glasses with stems, and a recipe for a meal that will make her guests feel honored . . .

A WOMAN SHOULD HAVE . . .
A feeling of control over her destiny . . .

EVERY WOMAN SHOULD KNOW . . .
How to fall in love without losing herself . . .

EVERY WOMAN SHOULD KNOW . . .
How to quit a job, break up with a lover, and confront a friend without ruining the friendship . . .

EVERY WOMAN SHOULD KNOW . . .
When to try harder . . . and when to walk away . . .

EVERY WOMAN SHOULD KNOW . . .
That she can't change the length of her calves, the width of her hips, or the nature of her parents . . .

EVERY WOMAN SHOULD KNOW . . .
That her childhood may not have been perfect . . . but it's over . . .

EVERY WOMAN SHOULD KNOW . . .
What she would and wouldn't do for love or more . . .

EVERY WOMAN SHOULD KNOW . . .
How to live alone . . . even if she doesn't like it . . .

EVERY WOMAN SHOULD KNOW . . .
Whom she can trust, whom she can't, and why she shouldn't take it personally . . .

EVERY WOMAN SHOULD KNOW . . .
Where to go . . . Be it to her best friend's kitchen table . . . Or a charming inn in the woods . . . When her soul needs soothing . . .

EVERY WOMAN SHOULD KNOW . . .
What she can and can't accomplish in a day . . . A month . . . and a year . . .

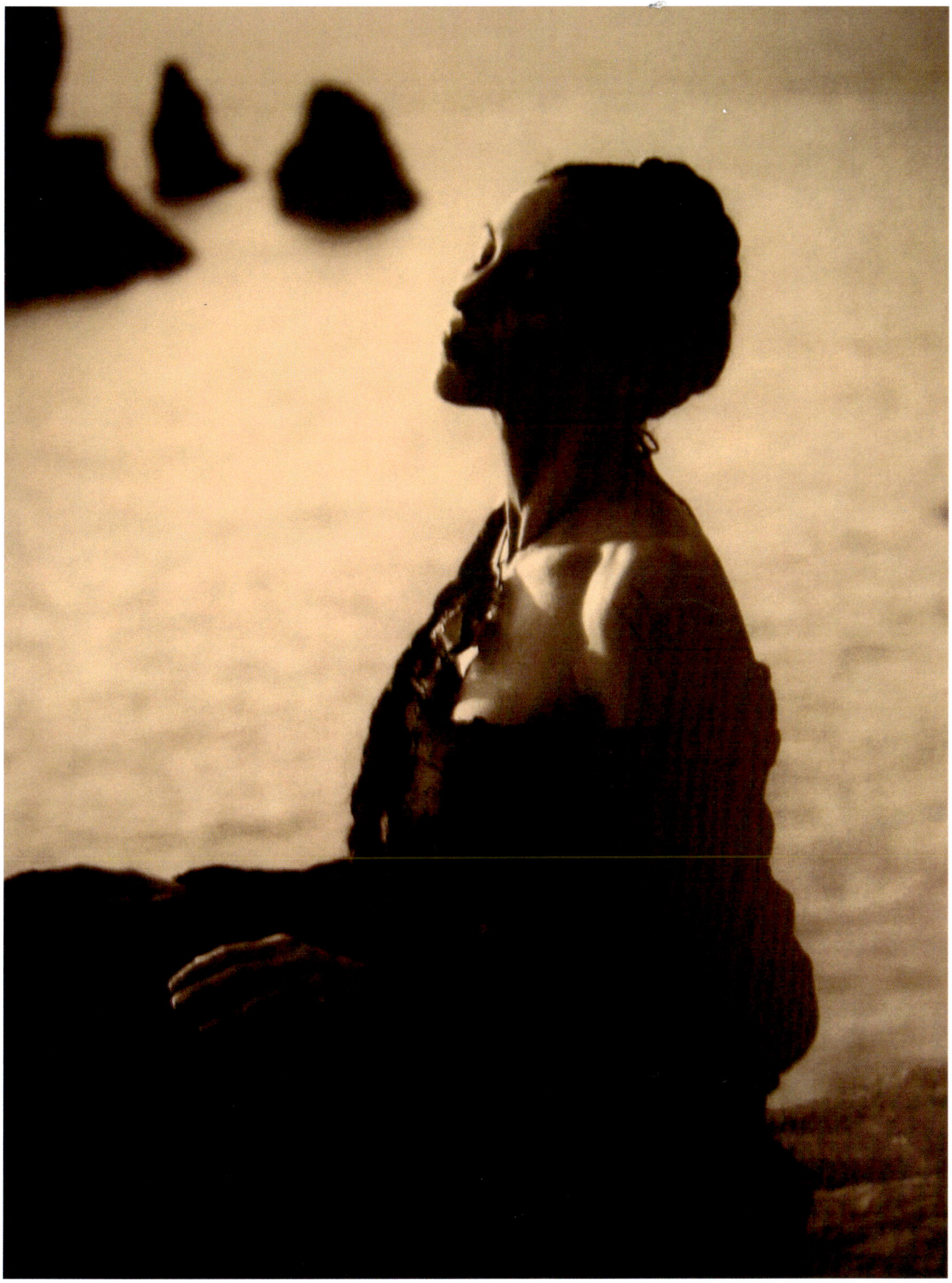